The Third Invention
How the Bow & Arrow Made History

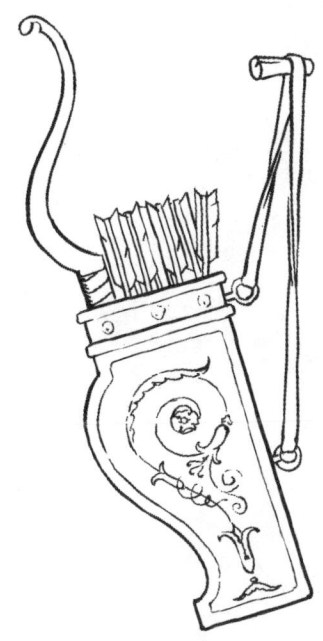

The Third Invention
How the Bow & Arrow Made History

by **Steve Hayes**

Introduction by Peter Ueberroth

Illustrations by Ned Dameron

A **HAMMERSMITH** BOOK
An imprint of Underwood-Miller
Novato, California
Columbia, Pennsylvania
1990

The Third Invention
How the Bow & Arrow Made History

Library Edition: ISBN 0-88733-086-X
Signed Edition: 087-8
Special Edition: 088-6

Copyright © 1990 by Steve Hayes
Illustrations Copyright © 1990 by Ned Dameron
Book design by Ted Pedersen

An Underwood-Miller book by arrangement with the author. No part of this book may be reproduced in any form or by any electronic or mechanical means including information storage and retrieval systems without explicit permission from the author or the author's agent, except by a reviewer who may quote brief passages. For information address the publisher: Underwood-Miller, 708 Westover Drive, Lancaster, PA 17601.

Printed in the United States of America
All Rights Reserved

10 9 8 7 6 5 4 3 2 1

Library of Congress Cataloging-in-Publication Data

Hayes, Steve, 1931-
   The Third Invention : how the bow and arrow made history / by Steve Hayes ; illustrations by Ned Dameron. -- 1st ed.
      p. cm.
   ISBN 0-88733-086-X : $39.95
   1. Bow and arrow--History.   I. Title.
GN498.B78H27   1990
799.2'15--dc20   89-20527
                                                                CIP

This book is dedicated to Cro-Magnon Man for inventing the bow and arrow . . . and to every man, woman and child thereafter who has enjoyed the sport of archery.

May all your arrows fly true.

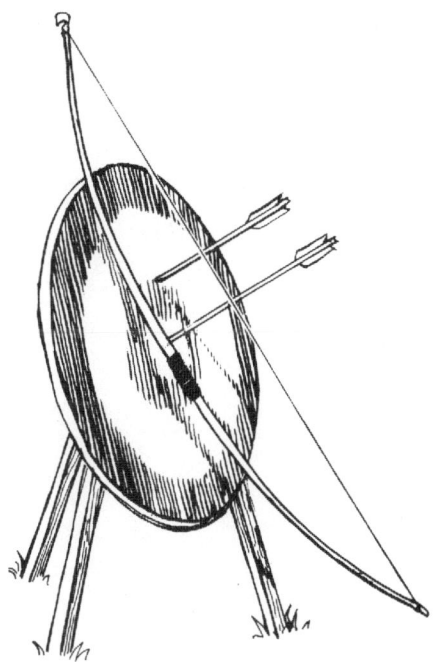

"By the drawing of the bow one can know the virtue and conduct of men."

Confucius

FOREWORD

No one knows exactly how or when Man first learned to control fire. The earliest hearths, dating back some 750,000 years, are in a cave at L'Escale, in southern France. But these fires were almost certainly not started by Man. There were no firestones, or traces of firestones, discovered in the cave—presently, the earliest known firestone dates back only 15,000 years—so it is pretty safe to assume that the fires at L'Escale were lit by live coals carried by Homo erectus from the overflow of an erupting volcano, or from burning grass set on fire by lightning.

But, whatever the date, Man's first true invention was fire. Once he learned how to create fire by striking certain rocks, such as flint and iron pyrites, together, he found his life changed forever. Fire enabled Homo erectus to cook his food, keep himself warm, ward off predators and light up the night.

Man's second true invention was the tool—for tools, like fire, significantly changed his life. And of all the tools Man invented, none was more valuable than the wheel. Again, no one knows for sure when or how Man created the wheel. But it is safe to say that, without it, he could not have transported anything larger than he could drag or carry, or built anything too substantial or lasting.

But Man needed to hunt to stay alive. And, wonderful as fire and tools were, they did not guarantee his survival in a world filled with creatures that were much larger, stronger, quicker, and more ferocious than any human being.

The responsibility of Man's survival as a hunter fell to a third invention—the bow and arrow. This simple but ingenious weapon "lengthened" the hunter's arm, enabling him to hunt from a distance and in comparative safety in a world inhabited by animals far better suited to hunting than Man.

But any weapon that could kill animals, could also kill human beings. Man was quick to discover this, and throughout history, he used the bow and arrow to defeat and kill his enemies.

Perhaps more than any other weapon, the bow and arrow was responsible for changing the course of history.

Steve Hayes

Acknowledgment

No book is ever a single effort. Many people contributed to this one. In particular I would like to thank Jim Easton for his support and the use of the Easton Sports Development Foundation Library; Joan Cohan of the West Los Angeles Public Library for supplying invaluable research material; Don Rabska and Toni Mench for always being there when I needed help.

Lastly, I would like to thank my wife, Robbin, for putting up with me during the two years it took to write this book.

CONTENTS

■ INTRODUCTION *1*

■ FOREWORD *3*

■ THE FIRST BOWHUNTERS *9*

■ THE FIRST AMERICANS *31*

■ THE ESKIMOS *43*

■ THE AMERICAN INDIANS *53*

■ THE ABORIGINES *65*

■ THE EGYPTIANS *77*

■ THE MACEDONIANS *91*

■ THE CHINESE *99*

■ THE PARTHIANS *109*

■ THE ANCIENT BRITONS *115*

■ THE ROMANS *127*

■ THE HUNS *137*

■ THE VIKINGS *151*

■ THE CRUSADERS *161*

■ THE MONGOLS *169*

- THE LONGBOWMEN *183*
- THE PORTUGUESE *197*
- THE TURKS *205*
- THE SOUTHERNERS *213*
- THE APACHES *219*
- THE ARROW MAKER *229*
- THE ARCHER *235*
- THE BUSHMEN *245*
- THE OLYMPIANS *257*

INTRODUCTION

I FIRST EXPERIENCED archery at a YMCA summer camp program in the Santa Cruz Mountains near my home in San Jose. I worked my way up to the top level of YMCA awards and went on to instruct archery at the camp. However, I grew to really appreciate competitive archery at the 1984 Olympic Games in Los Angeles.

The beauty and pageantry of the sport, the skill and dedication of the archers, and its long and colorful history impressed me.

Archery is one of the Olympic sports that is truly an amateur event in the spirit of past Olympics. It is a sport in which skill is more important than size. Men and women of any stature and of all ages can compete successfully in archery competion.

But more than being one of the oldest sports known, archery benefited humankind in many ways. Not only did it provide the means to feed themselves, but it became the way to defend territory.

Throughout the Human Adventure, the bow and arrow has played a major role. (Before gunpowder, the development of better bows and techniques would change the balance of power in the world.)

Like every important invention since the dawn of time, it is not the tool that was critical, but the innovative ways in which that tool was used. And that is what Steve Hayes has set out to illuminate in his book.

He has selected key historical "moments" that clearly illustrate how the bow and arrow won battles, changed lives, and altered destinies forever—thus shaping the world in which we find ourselves today.

During the past thirty years Steve's contributions as a champion archer, Olympic-caliber coach, technical equipment consultant, and National Archery Association board member has made him an acknowledged expert in the field.

His long love affair with archery is evident throughout the book. These twenty-four stories are not dry chronology, but human dramas based on historical fact—*docudramas*, as television likes to call them.

I hope you enjoy reading them as much as I did.

Peter Ueberroth

Peter Ueberroth was President of the Los Angeles Olympic Organizing Committee from 1979-1984 and Commissioner of Major League Baseball from 1984-1989.

The Third Invention
How the Bow & Arrow Made History

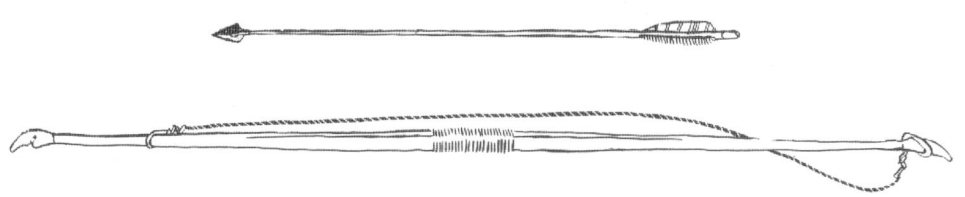

Archaeological evidence indicates that the first men to enter the North American continent emigrated from Asia. The easiest route from Asia to North America was across the Bering Strait that separated Siberia from Alaska. During the Upper Pleistocene ice age, when sea levels were lowest, the shallow strait became a land bridge that remained open for some ten thousand years. During this time Cro-Magnon hunters and their families, in search of food, crossed the land bridge on foot.

THE FIRST BOWHUNTERS

IT WAS DAWN and a cold, sleeting rain poured down from the wintry gray sky. Dark clouds gathered ominously overhead, and thunder could be heard rumbling above the distant snow-capped mountains.

But none of the men crouched behind rocks on the hillside cared about the approaching storm, or about the rain that blew in their faces and soaked the bear pelts draped over their powerfully muscled shoulders. They were hunters, and their only interest was the huge woolly rhinoceros grazing in the narrow, snow-dappled valley below.

There were only five hunters, for the Tribe of Grur was small, and each one knew he might be killed before their crude, stone-pointed spears downed the rhino. But this had been a long bleak winter and game was scarce, so they were grateful for food of any kind. At any risk.

The rhino, its massive, stubby-legged body covered with long thick hair to protect it against the harsh glacial cold that blanketed Europe during the Last Ice Age, was unaware of the hunters and kept its head lowered as it grazed on grass and scrub poking up through the frost-cracked earth.

The leader of the hunters, Grur, now signaled with his spear for his son and the others to follow him down the steep, rocky hillside. Although already old at forty-two, Grur was still a powerful man of five feet nine, with long dark hair, an unkempt beard and intelligent brown eyes that peered out from under strongly developed, but not Neanderthal, brows. Like the other hunters, Grur wore a loose, sleeveless jacket and loincloth made of bear pelts, and his feet were wrapped in deerskin tied around the ankles with sinew. About his neck hung a rawhide thong decorated with shells and lion teeth, and tucked into his loincloth were a bone dagger and a wooden handled stone axe. The spear he carried had a stone point that Grur had chipped until it was flint-sharp, and then bound it to a wooden shaft with sinew.

When the hunters reached the bottom of the hill, they were within fifty paces of the woolly rhino. But the beast had poor eyesight and the downwind hunters knew they would be safe until they were much closer, or some noise betrayed their presence.

Usually, the hunters tried to drive dangerous animals like rhinos or mammoths into a marshy area, trapping them in the mire and slaughtering them with spears. But since the ground was frozen and covered with patches of snow, the hunters had no choice but to get close to the rhino, then try to kill it before the enraged beast trampled them to death or impaled them on its two deadly horns.

Using rocks and leafless scrub as cover, the hunters moved quietly up behind the unsuspecting woolly rhino. When they were within twenty paces, Grur motioned for his son, Yud, to stay behind him. But Yud, a tall, muscular boy in his early teens, was anxious to prove himself to the seasoned hunters. Ignoring his father, he fitted his spear into a spear-thrower and hurled the weapon at the still-grazing rhinoceros.

The spear struck the rhino behind the left shoulder and despite the thick, matted hair sank in past the stone point. The surprised beast grunted in pain, whirled around, snorting, and looked with piggy, bloodshot eyes for its attacker.

Yud gave a savage cry of triumph, and yelled for the other hunters to throw their spears. Before they could, the woolly rhinoceros lowered his head and charged them. Everyone scattered before the pain-maddened beast, barely avoiding its horns as the rhino galloped past. Then, as the rhino whirled and charged again, the hunters bravely formed a half-circle and hurled their spears at it.

Two of the spears buried into the massive curved neck of the charging rhino; the others hit bone and bounced off. The rhino thundered on, unfazed by the spears, and came straight at Grur.

He turned and ran toward some nearby rocks. The enraged rhino, surprisingly nimble for its immense size, changed directions without slowing and charged after Grur.

It quickly gained on him. Yud, seeing his father about to be trampled, darted in front of the charging rhino, yelling and waving his hands to attract the beast's attention. Without slowing, it swung its lowered head at Yud. He jumped aside. But he was not fast enough and the long, curving front horn hooked the boy in the groin. He screamed, once. The rhino then tossed its head so that the horn sank deeper into Yud's groin, up through his stomach and out his chest, impaling him; and not stopping, still running in that quick, choppy, stubby-legged motion, the spears in its arched hairy neck flopping at each step, the dead boy held aloft on its bloodied horn.

Horrified, Grur and the other hunters picked up their spears and ran after the rhino. It stopped after a short distance and tossed its head again, flipping Yud's mangled corpse from its horn. Then it rubbed its neck against some rocks, tearing the spears loose and leaving bloodstains on the icy stone. The rhinoceros then trotted away, head lowered, its massive body swinging from side to side, its short hairy tail held high in triumphant defiance.

The Tribe of Grur lived in a cave in a limestone cliff beside a shallow, fast-moving river. It was a clean cave with a narrow, sheltered opening that kept out the wind. Inside, was a large flat-floored room with a high arched ceiling in which was a small opening that allowed the smoke to escape. The rear of the cave narrowed into a tunnel that ended in a small chamber that had natural ventilation and—Grur realized on discovery—would be perfect for burials. In a shallow pit in the middle of the mainroom, a smoldering fire was kept alight day and night, the women piling on extra wood whenever flames were needed for cooking.

Spears and clubs hung on the smoke-blackened walls, along with stretched-out hides that were drying for later use.

Grur had found the cave four years ago. He was hunting with his wife's three brothers, when a sudden electrical storm forced them to look for shelter. Terrified by lightning bolts, they ducked behind some nearby rocks—Grur discovering that his rock hid the entrance to a cave. Half-expecting to be attacked by a lion or a bear, the hunters warily entered the cave and explored it until the storm abated. Then, impressed by its ventilation, size and nearness to the river, they returned to the cliff overhang they had been living under, collected their respective families and personal belongings and moved into the new cave.

For four years the Tribe of Grur lived comfortably in the cave. Game was plentiful, fish easily caught in the nearby river, and all their babies were born without defects. The tribe flourished. It was a time of much joy.

But now, as Grur stood in the funeral chamber beside his son's grave, he was too grief-stricken to remember the good times. In his own quiet way he'd been enormously proud of Yud, and loved him more than life itself. And now the boy was gone forever.

Equally saddening, Grur also knew he was approaching the end of his life and that it was too late to sire any more sons; which meant his wife and two young daughters would have to survive without a man in the family, not a pleasant thought to take to his grave. But life was like that. Long ago Grur had learned there was nothing he could do to appease the gods, or change what they had planned for him.

So, eyes stinging with tears, he kneeled by the open grave and with trembling fingers placed Yud's weapons across the dead boy's chest. A pelt of a cave bear was added, along with food, fresh firewood and flints to accompany the young hunter on his unknown journey. Then, satisfied he'd done all he could to make Yud's life after death comfortable and safe, Grur rose and placed a rock on his son's body.

Other members of the tribe now entered, each placing a rock on Yud's corpse until the grave was covered. Then everyone left but Grur's wife, Ayr—a small, thick-limbed, stoic woman of forty who took her place beside the grave. Eyes closed, hands palm-down on the grave, she began her all-night vigil to make sure nothing disturbed her son's departing soul.

Outside, alone in the darkness, Grur stood looking at the moon. Its shape resembled the horn of the woolly rhinoceros that had killed Yud. Grur wondered why the gods had taken a boy just starting manhood when he, Grur, was so close to death himself. Perhaps, he thought hopefully, it was the gods' plan to let him meet with his son again in another place. But Grur could not convince himself of this and, heavy hearted, he wandered aimlessly toward the river. The shallow water was icy around his legs and the current swift, but Grur barely noticed.

Nor did he notice the swirling storm clouds darkening overhead.

All he could think of was that he'd never see Yud smile again, or hear his happy laughter echoing in the cave.

Grur wandered on, mind churning. Thunder now crackled overhead and lightning flashed in the sky above the forested, snow-capped hill ahead. Normally, Grur and the other tribe members were frightened of the lightning god; tonight, it seemed to be beckoning Grur on—as if it wanted him alone, so it could share with him the secrets of life after death.

Rain suddenly beat on him, and high gusting winds whipped his long tangled hair across his bearded, weathered face. He ignored the storm and, without really knowing why, started up the steep hill. The wind grew stronger and stronger—until its howling filled Grur's ears and its force almost blew him off his feet.

As he climbed higher, saplings alongside the narrow winding trail were bent over by the wind until their branches scraped the dirt. But not one of them broke. Unlike the great oak tree that

Grur saw torn out of its roots and hurled across the trail ahead of him, the saplings whipped back to their original shape and remained rooted in the earth. More than that, when windblown debris landed on the branches of the bent saplings and the trees whipped back to their upright position, the debris was hurled away with great velocity. Grur had seen the same thing happen occasionally in other forests during other storms, but this was the first time he really took notice of it; and as he continued climbing, he stored the knowledge away as if knowing some day it would be important.

When he finally reached the snowy crest of the hill, the storm had started to move on and Grur felt the wind slackening around him. He sniffed, testing the night air for danger. It contained no animal scents. He filled his lungs with its cool freshness. The air smelled of rain-soaked trees and of the wet fur covering his shoulders. Weary, but strangely exhilarated, Grur sat on a rock and watched the dark thunderheads swirling across the gleaming moon. Their eerie drifting shapes fascinated him and more than once they seemed to form the face of his dead son. Uneasy, he wondered if this was what the lightning god had brought him up here for: to let him see Yud a final time; to teach Grur that all men—and probably animals, too—became clouds when they died. The idea was not dismaying. Clouds were free and seemed to have fun chasing each other across the sky.

Pleased with his thoughts, Grur felt the pain in his heart ease a little; and after sitting there a while, he felt well enough to face life again, as well as his wife and the others in the tribe. Rising, Grur thanked the lightning god for sharing his infinite wisdom and started down the hill to the cave.

That night the image of the wind-bent saplings filled Grur's dreams. And when he waked the next morning, he talked to the other hunters around the breakfast fire. If they were to stay alive while hunting he explained, they needed a weapon that could kill their quarry from afar; perhaps even from behind cover. Everyone agreed that Grur was right. But no one had any suggestions about how to make such a weapon.

"Follow me," was all Grur said. He led the puzzled men outside. There, by the river, he chose a young sapling that he could bend over and tied it down with a vine. Then he put a rock atop the branches and cut the vine with his stone knife.

The sapling sprang back to its original position, hurling the rock with such force against the outside wall of their cave that the rock shattered.

"This is how we'll kill dangerous animals from now on," Grur told his impressed followers. "From a safe distance. . .even behind cover, when it's available. And once we learn how to be accurate, none of us will be injured or killed again." But it wasn't that easy. The hunters practiced hard during the following weeks, but they never learned to hurl the rocks accurately. One or two animals in a large herd could be killed by a bombardment of hurled rocks, but their death was more by luck or density of numbers than due to the skill of the rock-throwers.

Disappointed, Grur and the other hunters finally gave up on the idea and returned to hunting with their spears. But Grur never stopped thinking about the flexible saplings; nor about the tribe's need for a weapon that could kill game from a safe distance.

Spring came and with it, another tragedy. A marauding cave lion attacked the tribe one afternoon. It was hot and windless and the children, cooped up in the cave for most of the winter, were playing with pebbles in the sun outside the cave. The huge, maneless lion was among them before anyone realized. It mauled two of the older children, then, unnerved by their screaming, bounded off with one of the infants between its jaws. Her screams and the screams of the other children brought everyone running. But when they reached the cave mouth, the lion was already out of spear range. The enraged hunters hurled their spears anyway, watching in helpless frustration as the weapons fell short.

The father of the infant, Worg, raised his fists and screamed abuse at the heavens. Worg was the largest, strongest man in the tribe. In his teens he'd lost his left eye in a fight with a cave bear, and a long ugly white scar twisted the whole side of his face into a perpetual scowl. His semi-blindness made him wary and bad-tempered, and he often beat his wife and the other women of the tribe at the slightest provocation. At thirty-one Worg was three years older than his twin brothers, Chak and Var. They were also smaller and less aggressive, and well-liked by the rest of the tribe. Their older sister, Ayr, was Grur's wife—something that constantly rankled Worg. He was jealous of Grur, felt that he and not Grur should lead the tribe, and made no effort to hide his resentment.

Now, distraught at the loss of his daughter, Worg showed his disrespect for Grur's leadership by not waiting for orders, and instead picked up his spear and ran after the cave lion. His brothers looked uneasily at Grur, waiting to see his reaction.

Grur wisely stored away Worg's insult, signaled for Var and Chak to pick up their spears and led them after Worg.

As he ran, Grur wondered why the gods refused to show him a way to make a weapon that could kill from a distance. With such a weapon he could have stopped the cave lion from snatching Worg's daughter; or, at the very least, wounded the big cat so that it was less formidable when the hunters tried to kill it with their spears. As it was, the cornered lion would probably wound or kill some of them. That would weaken the already small, predominantly female Tribe of Grur and make it impossible for them to survive without joining another tribe. Grur was against this. He was proud of the tribe's independence, and fiercely determined to show everyone that under his leadership they were not just surviving, but flourishing. So far, he had succeeded.

But now, this cave lion hunt could undo everything Grur had worked so hard to achieve. It was a depressing thought, and as Grur led Chak and Var after Worg, he grimly made up his mind to do whatever it took to keep himself and the others alive.

The hunters knew there was little hope of rescuing Worg's daughter, but to a man they were determined to revenge her death by killing the lion. They followed its tracks, and the trail of occasional blood spots, east across the rock-studded hills. The hills sloped down to a small green meadow that was fringed by a dense forest. A stream came out of the forest, curved through the meadow and disappeared into a thicket of willows.

The hunters stopped on a hillside overlooking the meadow.

The sun was dipping below the horizon and its last rays flooded the pale blue sky with streaks of red and orange.

"There!" Worg pointed. Grur and the other hunters looked. The cave lion was crouched on the bank among the willows, drinking from the stream. Worg's daughter lay, lifeless, beside it.

"Hurry," Worg said, already scrambling down the hill. "Before it grows dark and we lose the lion in the forest." It took the hunters ten minutes to reach the willows. By then, the lion was gone. So was the body of Worg's daughter. Kneeling on the flat rock, Worg wiped his fingers in his daughter's blood. Next he pulled his bearskin aside and smeared the blood over his chest. It was his primitive way of placing his daughter nearest his heart. Comforted, he remained on his knees for a moment, eyes closed, waiting for his daughter to join souls with him. Tears ran down his lined, weathered cheeks into his beard.

Watching him, Grur was touched. He was not overly fond of Worg, but he empathized with his brother-in-law's grief and at that moment wanted to kill the cave lion more than anything.

Spear in hand, he plunged deeper into the willows. Dense curtains of hanging branches, their thin green leaves reaching to the ground, blocked his path. He brushed them aside, one after another, their sheer numbers impeding his progress. He could hear Worg, Chak and Var following close behind. Ahead, the snarling, deep-throated roar of the cave lion suddenly echoed out of the forest. It was closer than Grur expected.

For a moment, fear chilled him. He knew the willows grew along the bank of the stream right into the forest and that the lion could be hiding anywhere among them. He also knew that he would not see the lion before he was almost on top of it, and had to be instantly ready to hurl his spear. With this in mind, Grur changed the spear into his throwing hand and held it butt-end first, so that when he cocked his arm the spear would be ready to throw. He'd had the spear for two seasons. He called it "Wa-nu-eena", which was the best kind of good luck, and Grur knew if he aimed it well it would not let him down. The leaf-shaped stone point was so sharp, it drew blood at the lightest touch; and the shaft, cut from a thick elm branch, would not break if he had to use the spear as a stabbing weapon. It was a comforting thought, especially when hunting cave lions, and Grur felt better as he pressed on through the willows.

Shortly, the willows began to thin out. Other trees and tall bushes with slender, whippy branches took their place.

Grur realized he had reached the edge of the forest. It was darker here. As he walked, he looked up and saw the branches overhead formed a leafy ceiling that blocked out the light.

This made it almost impossible to see the lion, and Grur knew it was time to order everyone to turn back before one or all of them were killed.

Suddenly the butt-end of his shaft, which although trimmed still had the base of a V-shaped twig attached, snagged on the branch of a big bush. The branch bent back under the momentum of Grur's forward stride and then whipped back to its original upright position, similar to a wind-bent sapling, hurling the spear behind Grur.

Grur turned, pushed aside the still-swinging branches behind him and saw that his spear had buried in a nearby tree trunk.

Stopped within inches of the spear was Chak, a shocked expression on his youthful tanned face.

"Why'd you throw your spear at me?" he demanded angrily. "You could have killed me, Grur!"

"It was an accident," Grur began. He stopped as the lion roared again, dangerously close now, but still hidden by the trees. Grur pulled his spear from the trunk and waited for Worg and Var to join them. "It's coming for us," he whispered. "You three keep hidden, and I will act as bait." He waited until Worg, Chak and Var had ducked behind nearby trees, then moved into a tiny clearing. Keeping his back protected by a big oak, Grur kneeled on one knee. Next he buried the shaft-end of his spear in the dirt and held the point out before him.

Waited.

Seconds, that seemed like minutes, dragged by. Grur could hear the blood pounding in his ears. He squinted in the half-light. He couldn't see the lion but knew instinctively it was close. He tightened his grip on the shaft of the spear.

Waited.

Another tense moment passed. Then Grur heard faint, stealthy rustling among the bushes across the clearing. Good, he thought. The gods are with me this time. They are making the lion come straight at me.

Even as Grur thought, the cave lion sprang out of the bushes. It came in a rush. Fast. Almost too fast to believe. Roaring.

A sudden, heart-stopping, blood-chilling leap, the huge tawny body with its jaws open, fangs bared, outlined against the dark green-brown of the forest. There was no time to act; no time to even think. For one instant Grur saw the lion hurtling down toward him, claws extended in its out-stretched front paws; the next, it had impaled itself on Grur's upright spear.

The spear drove right through the lion's chest, up and out its back between its shoulders. But Grur never saw it. For the full weight of the lion struck him, head-on, knocking him sprawling.

He lay where he fell, stunned. The roaring of the dying lion filled his ears, but seemed to come from far-off. Distant but immediate. Vague shapes floated in and out of Grur's ground-level vision. Grur blinked. The haze cleared and he saw Worg, Chak and Var plunging their spears again and again into the body of the writhing lion.

Finally, it was over. The lion lay dead in its own blood.

None of the hunters were even scratched. They stood in the fading dusk, heads bowed, and gave silent thanks to the god of the hunt for sparing their lives. The killing of a cave lion, the largest feline to ever roam the earth, was a great feat under normal circumstances. And but for the loss of Worg's daughter, the hunters would have celebrated. But now, after a moment's elation, the four primitive men solemnly hunkered down and began skinning out the lion. Afterward, they would quarter the meat, making it easier to carry back to the cave.

"We'll camp here for the night," Grur instructed the others. "Then, tomorrow, we'll try to find the body of Worg's daughter before returning to the cave." He looked at Worg as he spoke, wondering if his brother-in-law would challenge his authority.

Worg didn't. He avoided Grur's stare and said nothing as he used his stone scraper to peel the skin from the lion's belly.

"Well-spoken," Var said respectfully to Grur. "Today you have proved once again that you are a great leader."

"And a mighty hunter," Chak said, adding: "When we get back to the cave, I will use my brightest colors to paint this hunt on the walls...so that our children, and the children of all future hunters, may also know of your greatness." Grur, knowing it was rude to acknowledge praise, did not say anything. But as he continued skinning one of the lion's huge forepaws, he felt good inside; and not so old or threatened by Worg's younger, stronger, challenging presence.

The next morning, at first light, they cooked hunks of lion meat over the fire. They ate the charred pieces by holding one end in their teeth and cutting off a mouthful with their stone knives.

When they were finished, they wiped their greasy hands on their thighs and drank from the stream. They then slung the quartered chunks of cave lion over their shoulders and searched the forest for the remains of Worg's daughter.

They found traces of blood, and a piece of blood-stained fur that the infant had been wearing, but nothing else. Worg was heart-broken but did not argue when Grur ended the hunt and led them out of the forest.

It took Chak two days to prepare the area on the wall he had chosen at the rear of the cave to paint the cave lion hunt.

The surface of the rock was moist and the young artist spent several hours drying it out with a burning torch. Then, satisfied it was dry enough to accept his various pigments, Chak rubbed the fire-blackened rock clean with deerskin and sanded it smooth with a limestone. It was an arm-wearying task. But when he was finally finished, the rock was clean and its surface had a grainy, porous texture that absorbed the colors and prevented them from blurring. Chak was now ready to sketch the various scenes of the hunt as he remembered them. Using a crude animal hair brush dipped in black pigment, he carefully outlined the four hunters stalking through the willows. Later, when all the scenes were finished, he would color them in with red, yellow and brown pigments that he kept separate in ancient sea shells.

In the ensuing days and nights, Grur and the other members of the tribe watched the scenes depicting the lion hunt evolving on the cave walls with a mixture of awe, envy and childlike joy. None of them could draw or paint as well as Chak, and they marveled at his artistic ability to depict animals and hunters in such lifelike action, they seemed to be alive; especially at night, when the flickering firelight cast eerie moving shadows on the walls, making the figures seem to come alive.

Grur was as awed and pleased with Chak's painting as anyone.

In the evenings he sat near the fire, his back propped against the wall opposite the paintings, and watched his brother-in-law working on the realistic mural. Grur's eyesight was failing, and he had to squint in order to pick out each detail of the hunt. Sometimes, weary from a day of hunting and with his belly bloated by the evening meal, Grur dozed off. Most of the time, he was not aware of falling asleep. Nor would he remember, upon awakening, that he'd been asleep. And as he rubbed his sleep-blurred eyes and saw the shadowy paintings flickering on the wall opposite, he'd give an alarmed grunt and reach for his spear as protection. Then he'd hear the children giggling at him from their bedding, and, embarrassed, he'd sheepishly realize that it was just a painting.

One morning, Chak sketched a scene that seemed unrelated to the lion hunt. It showed himself being narrowly missed by Grur's spear. Ayr saw the scene first and angrily accused Chak of trying to degrade her husband. She ran to Grur and demanded that he order Chak to erase the scene. Grur studied the drawing for a moment, puzzled. Then, remembering the incident, he laughed and described to the tribe members now gathered about him how the near-fatal accident occurred.

Worg saw this as a chance to weaken Grur's credibility in front of the tribe, and accused Grur of being too old to hunt safely. Either that Worg added, when he saw no one believed him, or Grur was lying. No bush could hurl a spear.

Angry, Grur held his temper and led everyone outside. They walked until they found a suitable bush. Grur then chose the most pliable limb, held the end of Var's spear against it, bent the limb back and let go. The spear was hurled fifty feet.

Happily surprised by his success, Grur retrieved the spear and tried again, this time aiming at a tree fifty paces away.

The spear not only hit the tree but stuck in the trunk so firmly, Grur broke the shaft trying to pull it loose.

There were grunts of shocked amazement from the tribe. They crowded around Grur and congratulated him. Only Worg remained outwardly unimpressed. Inwardly he knew Grur had stumbled upon an important weapon, and was as impressed as everyone else.

Pleased by his success, Grur told Chak and Var to fire their spears from the bush. They did, suspiciously at first and then eagerly as, in succession, both showed how accurate a launched spear was when properly aimed.

But Worg, jealous of Grur's success, belittled the weapon. He argued that there weren't always going to be suitable bushes or trees growing beside the game trails. He was right, Grur had to admit. But, unlike the others, who shrugged their shoulders and gave up on the matter, Grur sat alone by the fire and thought of nothing else.

Days passed. Grur spent every waking moment thinking of ways to improve his new weapon, but it was useless. He grew moody and depressed. He ate little and snapped at everyone, including his wife. Finally, he returned to the hill where he had locked minds with the lightning god, hoping for inspiration.

It was late Spring now and the grassy hill was bright with wild flowers. Grur trudged up to the forest. On both sides of the trail the saplings stood tall and slender in the warm sunshine. Please help me, Grur begged the lightning god. I know this new shooting weapon is important to the tribe's survival, but I can't find a way to make it practical. Then, because it was sunny and Grur was a logical man, he made the same prayer to the sun god.

Suddenly, Grur stopped. Across the trail before him lay the huge oak that the wind had uprooted during the storm. The oak was many times larger than any sapling, but because it could not bend, Grur knew the wind god had killed it. It was a lesson that Grur had learned many times during his life: adapt or die! Grur looked at the gnarled, fallen tree for a moment, hoping he might learn from it. In the weeks the oak had lain there, Nature had already started absorbing the dying tree back into the land. Millions of termites were attacking the torn roots and decaying underside; while a woodpecker hopped along the trunk, pecking at a scattered column of ants that were retreating across the upcurled, yellowing bark.

Grur started to climb over the fallen tree—when it suddenly dawned on him: what he needed to make his new shooting weapon practical was to find an uprooted or "moveable" tree.

Translating this to mean a branch, Grur cut a six-foot limb from a nearby tree and trimmed off the excess twigs. He next buried the thicker end in the dirt, held his spear against the branch and bent it back. The pressure of bending the top of the branch pulled it out of the ground. Grur buried it deeper. Tried again. The released branch whipped forward, but with much less strength than when it was still on the tree. The spear was hurled only a short distance. Grur tried other branches, but the results were always disappointing: either the branch came out of the ground, or it didn't have enough strength to hurl the spear an acceptable distance. Dejected, but not defeated, Grur headed back to the cave.

What he needed he realized as he trudged along, was a way of holding the branch so that it behaved the same way as when it was on the tree. But what way was that? Perhaps if he wedged the branch between two rocks, or—. A sudden thought hit him.

What if someone held the branch in his hands while he, Grur, shot his spear from it? That would keep the branch steady, and at the same time enable the shooter to aim the spear at whatever target they wanted to hit. It sounded feasible; even practical.

Now all Grur needed was someone strong enough to hold the branch.

He immediately thought of Worg. But he knew Worg would never help him—no matter how good the idea was. He would have to outsmart him, Grur realized as he neared the cave; somehow trick Worg into helping him.

Worg, Chak and Var were sitting on the river bank, sharpening their spears under a shade tree, when Grur reached the cave.

Joining them, he deliberately ignored Worg and told Chak and Var that he had discovered a mighty new weapon and needed their help to test it. Worg instantly became interested, as Grur knew he would, and followed them to a large open area in front of the cave. There, Grur had Var, the weakest of the brothers, kneel down and hold a branch he'd cut earlier from a sapling at the base with both hands. Grur then bent the top of the branch halfway back, held the notched end of his spear against it, supported the shaft with his free hand, and let go. The spear flew straight, but landed only twenty paces away. Grur pretended to be disappointed. He tried again, this time pulling the branch farther back. But Var wasn't strong enough to hold the branch and after a struggle, he fell backward under the pressure.

Worg laughed scornfully, and called Var a puny girl.

Grur ignored him and gave the branch to Chak. He was stronger than Var, and held the branch firmly while Grur bent it two thirds of the way back and shot the spear.

"Thirty paces," Worg said derisively as the spear landed in the dirt. "You call that a 'mighty weapon', Grur? Why, a boy of ten can throw a spear farther than that!"

Grur smiled inwardly, knowing Worg had taken the bait. "That's true," he admitted. "But do not blame my weapon. If a man were strong enough to hold the branch while I pulled it all the way back, the spear would fly farther than the eye can see."

"Give it here," Worg growled, unable to resist showing off.

He grabbed the branch from Grur. Kneeled. Held the base of the branch with both hands and feet. "Now, bend the branch as far as you can. Worg will hold it steady until it breaks".

Grur held the notched end of his spear against the top of the branch, pulled back and let go. The branch whipped forward and hurled the spear seventy paces. Chak and Var clapped their hands and hooted with delight. Worg wasn't so enthusiastic. He grudgingly admitted the new weapon showed promise, but again quickly found fault: what if they came upon game unexpectedly. There wouldn't be time for anyone to kneel down or get set. By then, the game would be out of range. So, what use was the new weapon?

Grur, ever truthful, admitted that Worg was right. What they needed he told the hunters, was to make a branch that was already bent and ready to use. That way, the spears could be hurled from it instantly. How did he intend to do that, Worg demanded. And at the same time make the weapon portable?

Grur hesitated, wondering how himself. Then he remembered the tied-down saplings and it dawned on him how to accomplish both demands: fasten sinew to both ends of a bent branch.

Too excited to explain, Grur pulled a length of sinew from his waist-pouch and tied it to one end of the "shooting stick", bent the branch into the same D-shape of the tied-down saplings, and fastened the sinew to the other end.

He held the shooting stick out at arm's length and pulled the sinew with the fingers of his free hand. When he released the sinew, the bow made a pleasant thrumming sound. Grur smiled.

He plucked the sinew again and listened, pleased by the musical "thrummmming." Then, he held the notched end of the spear against the sinew, pulled it back and released it without aiming at anything. The spear flew awkwardly, its length and weight too cumbersome for the bow, and landed only a short distance away.

Grur retrieved the spear and shot it again. Again he was disappointed by its lack of velocity and accuracy. And after several more shots Grur decided a shorter, lighter spear was needed. He led Worg, Chak and Var to the river and knelt at the bank where clumps of tall reeds grew in the shallows. He broke off one of the straightest reeds, cut it a little longer than his arm, bound his smallest scraping flint to one end as a point and shot the reed into the air. It flew faster and straighter than his spear and buried, point down, in the earth on the other side of the river one hundred paces away.

For one long silent moment, the hunters were too shocked to move. Then Grur gave an excited, triumphant shout, and held his new shooting stick up to the sky. Fervently, he thanked the sun god and the lightning god for helping him. Nearby, Chak and Var hugged each other and danced clumsily about, hooting and shouting Grur's praises to the heavens.

"Every man and boy must own a shooting stick."

Even Worg could find nothing negative to say. He just stood there, staring at Grur's shooting stick and shaking his head in stunned amazement.

Grur watched him a moment, heart pumping with elation. Then, knowing that the future of the Tribe of Grur rested on Worg's broad, muscular shoulders, he pushed the shooting stick into his hands.

"Try it, Grur," he said quietly. "Then, together, we'll find another branch and make you a shooting stick of your own."

"What about us?" Var asked, his arm still around Chak's shoulders. "Will you help us make shooting sticks, too?"

"Yes," Grur replied. He suddenly felt tired and very, very old. "Every man and boy in our tribe must own a shooting stick and learn how to use it. For only that way, will the Tribe of Grur... and their ancestors...survive."

Grur died of pneumonia the following year, and was buried in the funeral chamber beside his son, Yud. Buried along with all his other possessions were his bow and arrows. By now, every man and boy in the tribe had their own bows and arrows and were expert at using them to kill game.

As the tribe gathered ceremoniously beside the grave of their former leader, each hunter gave thanks to Grur for the important gift he'd given them: the shooting stick.

For although these primitive men had no way of knowing how the bow and arrow would benefit mankind for tens of thousands of years to come, they did understand that Grur's invention had "lengthened" their arm, enabling them to hunt with comparative safety in a world inhabited by larger, stronger and more ferocious creatures.

And for that, they were all truly grateful. Even their new leader, Worg.

As with all things in Man's prehistoric past, no one can say exactly when or how Man invented something. The bow and arrow are no different. Bows made of wood, horn or other organic materials deteriorated over thousands of years, leaving no trace of their existence; while the earliest known cave paintings that depict bow-hunting scenes only date back some 15,000 to 20,000 years.

Arrowheads made of wood, bone or horn also deteriorated into dust. But other arrowhead materials, such as stone, obsidian and flint, survived. And the earliest of these, found in Tunisia, date back almost fifty thousand years. They are expertly shaped and very functional, indicating that even then Man was already familiar with the bow and arrow.

THE FIRST AMERICANS

CRALL WAS DYING, but he was happy. At forty-six, he was very old for a Cro-Magnon man, and in the past few months acute arthritis had made him a serious burden to the clan. Now, as he lay on his bed of furs in the small round pit-hut, with its framework of mammoth bones covered by animal skins, Crall weakly raised up and looked at the four men gathered around the hearth before him.

"My time has come," he told them. "I shall not live through another night."

Two of the men, Chag and Erod, were Crall's sons. The other two, Bronk and Agar, were only related by marriage, both having married one of Crall's daughters. All four men tried to assure Crall that he would last through many more nights—Bronk appearing less distressed by the idea of the old man's death than the others—but Crall silenced them with a feeble wave of his hand. Before he joined his forefathers, he continued after a long pause, he had something of great importance to tell

31

them: earlier, while half-asleep, he'd had a vision. In it he saw the clan leaving the homesite where they had spent most of their lives, and following the vast grazing herds as they migrated to their winter pastures. The journey would be difficult and dangerous, and perhaps some of them would not survive it, but when it eventually ended they would find themselves in a strange distant land...a land of lakes and rivers...of vast plains and forests filled with unknown creatures of enormous size...of long summers and short, temperate winters...and, most importantly, a never-ending abundance of wild game.

The four listeners were shocked by Crall's weakly uttered words. But before they could question him, the old man fell back on the furs and within a few moments, was dead.

They buried Crall in the soft, marshy tundra that thousands of years later would be covered with sea water and known as the Bering Straits, and put wreaths of saxifrage and yellow poppies on the rocks marking his grave. His spears were buried with him, so he could hunt in the land beyond, but not his bow and stone-tipped arrows. Generations ago, when their forefathers lived in a land covered with trees, all hunters owned bow and arrows. Or so the legend went. But now, and for as far back as anyone could remember, they lived in treeless areas and could not replace each bow when, despite great care, it finally broke. As a result, the men had gradually regressed to bone-shafted spears and spear-throwers, the latter a short driftwood or bone handle with a hooked tip that in effect lengthened the hunter's arm and, in a whiplike motion, added to the range and impact of the thrown spear.

Crall's coveted bow and arrows were passed down to Chag. With them came a certain amount of authority—for the hunter who owned these deadly weapons was relied upon to supply the most game, and therefore considered Head Hunter. Bronk resented Chag having the title, since he was two years older and felt himself to be a better hunter. But clan customs had to be recognized, so all Bronk could do was voice his dissent, then sit in his hut and sulk.

There was no wife to weep over Crall, for she had killed herself one night five winters ago by crawling out into a snowy blizzard rather than be a crippled burden on the already near-starving clan.

So Crall's two daughters, Sarna and Meena, assumed their mother's obligations and remained by the grave all night to make sure that Crall's spirit was not harmed or captured by evil gods as it left their father's body.

While the young women kept their all-night vigil, the men of the clan gathered around the hearth in Crall's hut and discussed their dead leader's vision. Bronk, quarrelsome by nature, dismissed it as the ravings of a delirious old man. Why should they leave an area where they had lived safely since childhood to wander aimlessly after the migrating herds of caribou? It not only was foolish, it was extremely dangerous. They would be exposed to winter when it came, and without food or proper shelter they were certain to starve or freeze to death.

Chag and Erod also had doubts about leaving their homesite, but kept them hidden. Chag, at 28, was four years older than his brother, and the more restless of the two. Since childhood he had always wondered what was beyond the mountains that sheltered their valley and now felt the gods were urging him to find out. Erod, though less curious, loved his brother and without question went along with Chag's decisions. Together, they told Bronk that they trusted their father and believed his vision was a message from the gods to lead the clan to this land of plenty...and to live there forever in peace and comfort.

"And if the vision is false and there is no land of plenty," Bronk challenged, "what then?"

"We'll worry about that, then," Chag said. "Meanwhile, we will have at least tried to better our lives. And as leaders and fathers, we owe our children the opportunity to have the best life available." He turned to Agar, silent up till now, adding: "Do you agree?"

Agar, a large, quiet man three years older than Chag, nodded in agreement. Last winter his only brother had died in a snow storm, and ever since Agar had felt anger toward the valley and the gods who ruled over it.

"We have used up all our luck in this valley," he told Bronk bluntly. "It's time to move our families to new hunting grounds, where the gods will once more smile on us."

"Then, go. All of you," Bronk said angrily. "The family of Bronk stays!" Rising, he stormed out.

"Don't worry," Chag said, seeing Erod and Agar's concern. "Bronk will change his mind once he sees we are really going. He has no choice. No man can feed and protect his family, alone. Even if he were not to get sick or injured, it is too difficult. That is why our forefathers formed the clan—to survive."

Chag was right. Bronk, despite insisting that neither he nor his family were going anywhere, finally changed his mind and grudgingly accompanied the rest of the clan out of the valley.

Leaving the only home any of them had ever known was a painful, traumatic experience. Ahead lay unknown and probably dangerous territory, never before seen by man, and behind were all the familiar sights and comforts they had grown accustomed to and loved. It was enough to make even the stoutest of hearts, Chag's included, beat a little faster; and as they climbed over the last rise and looked back at the low rolling hills on either side of them, no one spoke a word.

Then, led by Chag, they plodded across the seemingly endless tundra, carrying everything they owned on their backs as they followed a vast caribou herd that was headed east. The caribou moved at a slow walk, often stopping for long periods to graze.

They seemed unaware of the people trailing them, only the animals at the tail-end of the herd even bothering to look in the clan's direction. It was early autumn now. During the cooler, ever-shortening days the women dug for edible roots and bulbs, while the men killed small game and birds to eat. All had agreed not to kill any of the caribou, since the gods might consider it bad luck to harm the very creatures that were leading them to better surroundings. But other game, such as wild horses, deer or the giant moose, *Cervalces*, with antlers towering eight feet above its massive, droopy head, they killed and ate without compunction. Occasionally packs of Dire wolves attacked the herd, cutting out the sick and weak stragglers, and causing the other animals to stampede. The wolves, though half again as large as their descendants, timber wolves, seemed wary of human beings and made no attempt to attack the clan.

At night, under the shimmering iridescence of the northern lights, the clan pitched their skin tents and slept while the caribou themselves bedded down on the tundra.

Gradually, golden autumn whitened into winter. The days got shorter; the nights longer. Bitter winds came howling out of the north, bringing snow flurries that melted as they touched the ground, then hardened into ice at night. The caribou moved more swiftly now, pausing less and less to eat, making it difficult for the women and children of the clan to keep up with them.

Finally, one night the men gathered about the council fire and decided not to try and keep up with the caribou any longer. They would erect pit-huts in the next available sheltered gully, and remain there throughout the winter and following spring. Then, in late summer, when the migrating herds moved east again the clan would accompany them for as long as weather conditions permitted before erecting another semi-permanent winter shelter.

"This way," Chag explained to the others, "we lessen our chances of getting lost or starving during the winter." Everyone was in accord except Bronk. When next spring came, he said, he wanted to return to the original homesite. When this was rejected, he demanded to know how long they intended to follow the migrating herds.

"For as long as it takes to find the place Crall envisioned," Erod replied.

"But that could be forever," Bronk grumbled.

"True," Agar admitted. "And if that's the case, then it will be up to our children, or our children's children to continue the search—indefinitely."

Bronk looked across the flickering flames at the others, and spat disgustedly into the wintry darkness.

"Once we were proud and mighty hunters," he said bitterly. "Now, we are nothing more than wanderers!"

The others disagreed. Wanderers had no destination, they reminded Bronk. They did. It just might take several lifetimes to find it.

By late the following afternoon, the clan had lost sight of the fast-moving herd. The caribou tracks led into a narrow, steep-sided gully that offered some protection from the wind and snow. Chag and the others agreed to make this their campsite. While the women and children dug four holes, each a foot deep and eight feet in diameter, the men went hunting.

Game was scarce. By dusk, they had killed a fox that was gorging itself on the remains of a ptarmigan; and Chag downed a startled arctic hare with one arrow. But that was all. Bronk, reminding the other hunters that they needed to stockpile meat in order to survive the oncoming winter, suggested they catch up with the herd and kill some of the caribou stragglers. The gods cannot be angry with us, he argued, because if we don't eat the weak and sick animals, the Dire wolves will.

His logic convinced the others. They hurried off after the caribou. They moved at a mile-consuming dogtrot, and by daybreak had caught up with the herd. A large, bob-tailed saber-toothed cat had already downed one unlucky straggler; the hunters circled the cat warily, and closed in on two weak, slow-moving caribou.

Chag's first arrow hit the smaller animal in the neck. It jumped, startled, and tried to run. It was too old and weak; it collapsed after a hundred yards and the hunters moved in and clubbed it to death. The second caribou turned and faced its enemies, head lowered, its great spread of antlers held threateningly at the approaching hunters. Chag circled the caribou and shot an arrow into its flank. The animal flinched in pain, but held its ground. Chag moved closer and aimed another arrow at the reindeer's heart. As he released the arrow, there was a sudden loud cra-ack—as the bow broke at the handle!

For a moment, the dismayed hunters forgot about the caribou and stared at the broken bow in Chag's hand. For the first time since anyone could remember, the clan of Crall was without a bow and arrows. Hunting from now on would be harder and take longer, and the number of successful kills would be much lower. It was a grim moment.

"The gods have punished us for breaking our word and

killing the caribou," Agar said, discouraged. Chag and Erod nodded in agreement, too dejected to speak.

"It's all your fault," Bronk told Chag. "None of this evil would have struck us if you hadn't insisted we leave our homesite." It was more than Chag could take. Whirling, he hit Bronk on the head with the broken bow. Stunned, Bronk sank to his knees. Erod and Agar pulled Chag away before he could strike Bronk again.

"Come," they urged him. "We must skin out the caribou before wolves smell the carcass and devour it."

Winter came, bringing driving snowstorms and shrieking winds that threatened to blow away the three small pit-huts that the clan had built in the sheltered gully. Only the heavy rocks, piled around each hut to hold down the bison hides covering the mammoth tusk framework, prevented the winds from scattering everything across the frozen wasteland.

Most of the time, everyone remained inside their huts. On days when weather permitted, the men went hunting in the snow.

They killed a few arctic hares and ptarmigans, both difficult to see in their winter white camouflage, but nothing else. Once they trailed an injured woolly mammoth, but lost the huge creature in a blinding snowstorm that chased the hunters back to their huts.

Erod, the only single adult in the clan, lodged with Chag, his wife, Lara, and their twin 8-year-old sons, Ombo and Traal. It was crowded and smoky inside the pit-hut, but warm enough to prevent them from freezing to death. Food was rationed, and when the lakes froze over, everyone drank melted snow. During the snowstorms, when it was impossible to go outside, the clan remained huddled in the warmth of their furs and skins and tried to forget the intense cold by sleeping.

Erod, when he couldn't sleep, used a sharp-edged flint to carve animals out of broken pieces of mammoth tusk. He was easily the best carver in the clan, and his ivory figures were very lifelike. Chag, his mind on the future, asked Erod to carve out the figure of a hunter shooting a bow and arrow.

"This way," he confided to Erod, "we'll have a record of what a bow and arrow look like, should it be years before we find any more suitable trees." Pleased with the finished results, Erod pierced a hole in the hunter's body, strung sinew through it and gave it to Lara as a present. She was delighted. And the first time the weather cleared, she hung the amulet around her neck and went out and showed it to the other wives. Envious, Sarna and Meena begged Erod to carve similar amulets for them to wear. Erod agreed. But he only had one small piece of tusk left, and after finishing Sarna's carving, Erod realized he needed more ivory to carve a figure for Meena. She would have gladly accepted a bone carving, but Erod was an eccentric craftsman, who would only work on ivory. He told Meena that she'd have to wait until winter ended and he could find a dead mammoth or a broken tusk buried in the tundra.

At last, winter merged into spring. Green shoots poked through the snow; cracks appeared in the ice melting on lakes and ponds; and the winter white plumage of ptarmigans began turning a mottled red, brown and ocher.

The Clan of Crall emerged from their pit-huts with joyful hearts and empty bellies. Lara and Sarna had given birth to fat healthy sons, and Agar's wife, Meena, was only weeks away from delivery. Food was needed—and fast. The men went hunting. At first, it went badly for them. They had grown used to Chag's bow and arrow, and their accuracy with the spear-throwers had diminished. After returning empty-handed from their first few hunts, Agar remembered a method of hunting that his father had taught him. He scratched a plan in the dirt outside his pit-hut and Chag and the others agreed to test it out.

A few miles from their pit-huts, they piled dirt and rocks across the trail used annually by the migratory herds, hoping to force the animals into a nearby gully where they could trap them. Then, safely hidden behind some brush, the hunters lay in wait for the unsuspecting caribou.

Their timing was perfect. Shortly, a small herd approached, heading west for their summer pastures. The hunters waited until the caribou were close, then jumped up and began shouting and brandishing their spears.

The terrified caribou scattered. Some leaped over the dirt and rocks, while others panicked and ran alongside the wall until it ended at the brink of the gully. Unable to stop, the caribou plunged over into the gully. The hunters scrambled down after the caribou, relentlessly spearing the animals that hadn't already been killed by the fall.

Later, the Clan of Crall gathered about the camp-fire and gorged themselves on roasted caribou. "Today we learned two powerful lessons," Chag told the others. "As long as we remain together, we are strong, and will survive; and by using our minds, we can overcome any problem that threatens us. We must never be afraid to try new ways. Because if my father's bow hadn't broken, Agar might not have remembered this ancient way of hunting. . .and our future would've been uncertain." Turning to Bronk, he added: "Do you agree?"

"I agree that this way of hunting is good," Bronk said. "But I still believe it was a mistake to move from our homesite. For there, game was always plentiful and even without your father's bow, no one would ever have gone hungry."

"Nor will anyone ever go hungry when we reach the land that my father envisioned," Erod said, "for it was spoken that it was filled with animals."

"First, we have to reach there," Bronk said, disgusted. "And I, for one, don't believe we ever will." He rose and entered his pit-hut, leaving the others to finish the feast without him.

During the night, Erod heard a mammoth trumpeting. The beast sounded in pain, as if injured, and remembering his promise to Meena, Erod left the pit-hut and went looking for the mammoth.

He saw it limping slowly across a nearby frozen lake. It was an Imperial mammoth, the largest of its kind, and somehow it had injured both back legs. Halfway across the lake, its back legs gave out completely and the mammoth stopped, huge and pathetically misshapen in the moonlight, bellowing in agony. Then, using only its front legs, it tried to drag itself forward.

Erod hurried across the lake after the mammoth. He soon caught up with it, and was within a few yards of the helpless, crippled beast—when the ice gave way and both Erod and the mammoth plunged into the icy water.

The mammoth thrashed helplessly around, trumpeting shrilly, then sank beneath the surface and drowned. One of its flailing legs crushed Erod's skull as he tried to swim to safety, killing him instantly. His body sank to the bottom of the lake and was never recovered.

The next morning, the Clan of Crall found Erod missing and wondered where he could have gone. Since he never returned, they concluded that he had wandered off and been killed. Tragic as his unexpected death was, no one in the Clan fully appreciated how anthropologically significant his presence in the Clan had been.

To do that, they would have needed to be able to see many generations into the future.

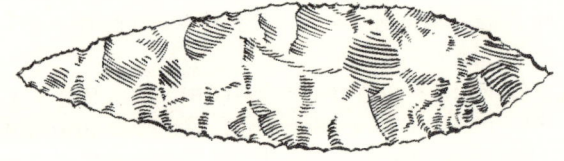

After crossing the Bering land bridge, Cro-Magnon men hunted along the icy, windswept coastline of northern Alaska. Seals, fish and other game were plentiful along the seashore and, despite the harsh environment and frigid Arctic temperatures, few hunters and their families were willing to head inland into the unknown and risk starvation.

But, generations later, some descendants of these families finally braved their way south, while others headed northeast and became...eskimos.

THE ESKIMOS

IT WAS AUTUMN and the Clan of Crall was temporarily camped in hide tents on the coast of North America bordering the Beaufort Sea. It should have been a time of happiness, full bellies and relaxation, but instead there was much concern: early freezing gales had driven the huge caribou herds south before their time and the Clan, new to the frigid coast and unprepared for such abrupt, unpredictable weather changes, hadn't stockpiled enough meat and fish to last through the winter. As a result, the men were forced to roam the barren, rocky coastline, hunting seals and spear-fishing, while the women and children looked for the eggs of sea birds that nested in the craggy cliffs overlooking the shoreline.

One evening, just before sunset, the weary hunters stumbled upon a rookery of seals. There were thousands of them, all sprawled on the rocks and pebbly beach. Led by the twin brothers, Traal and Ombo, the hunters separated a group of seals from the water and started spearing and clubbing them to death.

Panicked, the rest of the seals dove into the water, their cries deafening.

It was dark when the tired but excited hunters returned to camp, each man dragging several dead seals. Everyone ran out to greet them. The Clan was now fifty strong, and all except the infants helped cut up the meat and blubber. It was a moment of triumph and celebration, and everybody listened proudly as Traal, Ombo and the other young hunters recounted how the hunt went.

When the storytelling was over, and bellies were full, the elders gathered in the council tent to decide where they should spend the winter. Opinions were divided, and as usual the two leaders, Chag and Bronk, disagreed with each other. Chag, who was the father of Traal and Ombo, wanted to stockpile enough seal meat to last throughout the winter, then move inland and build their pit-huts in a sheltered spot near the mountain range that the migrating caribou herds crossed each spring and autumn. That way, he reasoned, the Clan would be already headed in the right direction when it came time to move on. Bronk, on the other hand, insisted they stay where they were; then, come spring thaw, the Clan could continue along the coast—where there would always be an abundance of fish and seals.

"But that would mean we're no longer following the migrating herds," Chag pointed out. "— something my father's vision said we must do in order to find our permanent hunting grounds."

Bronk made a scornful noise and looked into the faces gathered around the fire before him. He and Chag were the oldest and most respected members of the Clan and each had his loyal followers.

"I don't believe in Crall's vision," he said. "And I refuse to lead the Clan away from a constant supply of fresh food to some far-off place that only exists in the mind of a crazy, dying old man."

Bronk's followers were quick to agree, while Chag's supporters looked at their leader for his answer. Chag realized he was faced with a decision that would mean dividing the Clan.

"Ever since we left our original homesite," Chag said, including everyone but speaking directly to Bronk, "you and I have disagreed on almost everything. But one thing we never disagreed on, was splitting up the Clan."

"Nor do I wish to split it up now," Bronk said. "But if it means splitting up in order to save our lives, and the lives of generations to come, then split up we must. Because I cannot, in all good conscience, deliberately lead anyone to their death!"

The idea of actually splitting up the Clan disturbed everyone, and the arguing lasted deep into the night. But neither Chag nor Bronk would change their mind and it was finally decided to put the issue to a vote among all the hunters old enough to understand the seriousness of the situation.

The next morning, the vote was taken and the result was no surprise: Chag's followers voted to move; Bronk's, to stay. This forced them to form two clans, each about twenty-odd strong, each with blood relatives who were saddened by the idea of separating and never seeing one another again. But the decision had been made, and after two weeks of seal-hunting, the food and supplies were divided equally, tearful goodbyes were said and the Clan of Chag headed inland toward the mountains that, in future times, would be called the Brooks Range.

With winter fast-approaching, the Clan of Bronk built their pit-huts in a sheltered cove facing the sea. Because of the extreme arctic cold, the hunters over the years had learned to build the huts out of a dome of rocks braced by mammoth and whale bones. They had also found that by digging the inner pit deeper, and covering the rocks with an insulating layer of earth, they could keep warm even in extremely cold temperatures. Later generations would add an entrance passageway dug lower than the hut floor, to trap the cold air and prevent it from entering the living area, and fasten hides across the doorway to keep in the heat from the blubber cooking lamps. But for now, Bronk and his wife, Sarna, were content with their living quarters. In their early forties, they knew death was approaching and spent most of their days with their married children and grandchildren, trying not to be a burden on the Clan.

Bronk died late in December, when the arctic winds were at

their worst. He was buried in a shallow grave in the frozen ground, his weapons and personal possessions along with him, and within a month his grieving wife, Sarna, had died of a broken heart. She was buried alongside her husband, and mourned over by her three sons, daughter, and their grandchildren.

The oldest son, Drom, was made leader of the Clan of Bronk. Unlike his father, who had been sullen and stubbornly short-sighted concerning the Clan's future welfare, Drom was friendly, unselfish and open-minded when it came to any improvement or change that benefited everyone. It was this trait that enabled Drom to improve the Clan's hunting capabilities. On seeing the hunter-with-bow-and-arrow amulet that Erod had carved for Sarna and she had worn to her grave, Drom recalled how important the bow had once been to the Clan, and how dismayed the hunters were when Chag's bow broke during the caribou hunt. Although only a boy at the time, Drom vividly remembered everyone's consternation and how, because the environment offered no trees (and only a few bushes that were unsuitable for bows), the hunters had once more become deadly proficient with the spear-thrower. But one could only hurl a spear so far, even with a spear-thrower, and that distance was still short of the distance reached by a bow and arrow. It was also less accurate, and Drom spent hours every day wondering how a bow could be made without trees.

It came to him one winter's day when he was seal-hunting on the ice pack. Hunting had been poor lately, due mainly to the hunters' inability to get close enough to spear any seals that were seen out of the water. Until the spring thaw arrived to melt the ice and the seals returned to the beaches, the only partially successful form of hunting was to spear the seals as they surfaced to breathe in one of the numerous "breathing holes" in the ice. These holes were covered with a thin bubble of ice and if a man were patient enough, and could bear the frozen temperatures long enough to sit still for hours on end at one of these holes, then there was a chance he might spear a seal as it came up to breathe.

But even if he managed to spear the seal, that did not necessarily mean the hunter ended up with a kill. More often than not the spear didn't hit cleanly and the seal swam away, wounded but still full of fight, either breaking the spear or swimming off with it. Ropes of plaited sinew lashed to the shaft of the spear occasionally enabled the hunter to retrieve his weapon, but since barbed points had not yet been invented, the seals almost always swam away.

With these problems in mind, Drom found several short lengths of spruce driftwood and lashed them together with sinew. He also used sinew, stretched out over a blubber lamp until it would stretch no more, for a bowstring. Arrows he made from either driftwood or splintered mammoth bone, fletched with feathers from the ptarmigan and tipped with needlelike bones. The finished bow was about three feet long and very stiff, but after only a few shots it lost its resilience. Dismayed but undefeated, Drom lashed strips of chewed rawhide taken from the bearded seal to the back of the bow, and thin pieces of antler to the belly. Now the bow was even stiffer, and Drom guessed it would break before it lost any resilience.

Ready to test his new weapon, Drom went out onto the pack ice where he sat in frozen vigil by a seal breathing-hole.

Time dragged by. Freezing gusts of wind filled the air with swirling snow. The snow blew against Drom's face, but he was too cold and numb to feel it. Tiny icicles formed on his beard and on the fur fringe of his hood. With each breath he took, he felt the icy air numbing his lungs. It made breathing difficult and painful. Drom ignored the pain and forced himself to concentrate; to remember why he was there.

Finally, after several hours, he saw bubbles surfacing. A seal was approaching. Drom nocked an arrow with numbed fingers, drew back the string and aimed at the hole.

Moments passed. Then a bewhiskered black snout broke the surface as a seal gulped a lungful of air—and at that moment, Drom fired his arrow. It sank deep into the seal's open mouth and through its brain, killing it instantly. Blood reddened the water. The dead seal began to sink. Drom dropped his bow and picked up the length of sinew that was attached to the feathered

At that moment, Drom fired his arrow.

end of the arrow. Then pulling the dead seal to the surface, he grabbed it by the head and hauled the carcass onto the ice.

Forgetting how exhausted and cold he was, Drom gave a loud, triumphant shout. His new bow worked! Now, when spring arrived and the migratory caribou herds returned, the Clan would be able to hunt them more efficiently. That meant more meat for everyone, and a stronger, healthier Clan.

Elated, Drom slung his bow over his shoulder and headed back to camp, hauling the seal carcass behind him.

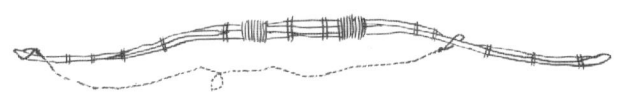

After leaving the north Alaskan coast and heading south, Cro-Magnon hunters were still blocked from entering North America by a colossal wall of ice that stretched almost coast to coast across Canada.

Intermittently, thousands of years apart, passages opened in this immense ice barrier. Most of them were just east of the Rockies, allowing hunters and their familes to pass safely through and enter the great plains of western Canada and North America.

Eventually, these men, women and children became the first American Indians.

THE AMERICAN INDIANS

THREE HUNDRED YEARS had passed since Chag was killed in a snowy avalanche near the Brooks Range. But the Clan—now called the Clan of Sangur—still remembered their remarkable leader in songs and campfire legends that had been handed down from generation to generation. Other stories and poems told of how Chag's twin sons, Traal and Ombo, had led the Clan across a great river that in the distant future would be named Mackenzie. The river wound through a broad valley that was flanked on both sides by enormous glaciers. At places the glaciers were no more than twenty-five miles apart, and, although the Clan did not know it, were inexorably inching closer and closer so that a few thousand years later the glaciers would join and form an unbroken barrier, a mile high at some places, stopping any more hunters from entering North America until 13,000 B.C.—when the glaciers retreated permanently.

The great caribou herds often used the valley as a means of reaching their winter pastures, and some of the older hunters in the Clan decided to go no farther and formed a settlement beside the river. The remainder of the Clan, led by Sangur, a distant descendant of Chag's, continued on through the valley in search of their permanent hunting grounds—a land of lakes and rivers, of vast plains and forests filled with game. . .of long summers and short, temperate winters that, legend had it, had been envisioned by Chag's father, Crall.

Sangur wasn't sure he really believed the legend, but he was an adventurous young man, too curious to remain in any place for long, and the vision's promise of seeing "strange creatures of enormous size" was lure enough to lead him on. Besides, since he was descended from Chag, and his wife Timmur wore around her neck the ancient ivory amulet carved by Erod, Sangur felt obligated to his ancestors to try to find a land with trees, so the Clan could again hunt with bows and arrows.

The search took several years, during which time the Clan of Sangur traveled the entire length of the glacier-flanked Mackenzie Valley and finally reached the vast open prairie that thousands of years later would be called Alberta. Here, where glaciers had long since retreated, roamed a veritable zoo of huge creatures. Mammoths and mastodons, 4,000 pound, armadillo-shaped glyptodons, giant bison, moose and deer, ground sloths that weighed three tons, saber-toothed cats and numerous other animals such as camels, lions, bears, beavers, wolves and wild horses. There were also lakes and rivers, but no forests. There was a scattering of coniferous trees, however, and Sangur and the other hunters used the branches to make bows. The best of the trees for bow-making were junipers, but even this wood lacked resiliency and broke when over-pulled. To add strength and resilience, the hunters backed their short, flat-limbed bows with strips of sinew. For arrows they used either reeds or thin branches straightened by pulling them through holes in hand-held stones. The needlelike bone tips were gradually replaced with stone arrowheads that were chipped to a razor sharpness. These changes were due to Sangur, who, having led the Clan to their permanent hunting grounds, now devoted his life to perfecting the bow for killing wild game.

Sangur also made every man and boy practice daily with their bows, and soon most of them were so skillful, they rarely missed their prey. This skill with the bow and arrow enabled them to drive off marauding bands of hunters who tried to steal the women. These small, predominantly male tribes were more scavengers than hunters. They had reached North America many years ago, but still had no knowledge of bows and arrows and despite their fierceness, were no match for the Clan of Sangur. But their constant attacks made life hazardous, especially for the women who now had to be guarded day and night.

One summer morning, while several of the women were fetching drinking water from a nearby river, the two hunters guarding them heard someone moving in the reeds. They shot arrows into the reeds, driving out a young, pale-haired girl whose face and body was badly bruised. Frightened, she started to wade across the river. But one of the hunters, Sangur's young brother, Moog, plunged in after her and caught her before she could reach the other bank. She fought him, biting and scratching, until he subdued her by holding her under the water until she almost drowned. Then, Moog dragged her ashore and threw her on the grassy bank in front of the Clan women. It took a while for her to recover and when she did, she cowed as if expecting to be beaten.

"What is your name?" Moog asked her. When she didn't answer, he repeated his question.

Unable to understand him, she turned to the women and pleaded with them to help her. She spoke in a tongue none of them understood, but her gestures made it obvious what she wanted and, taking pity on her, the women helped her up and led her back to camp.

The young girl's name was Ulva. Since Moog had no woman, and he had found Ulva, she was given to him. At first she was sullen and obeyed him only because she feared being beaten. But after a few days, when she realized Mood wasn't going to abuse her, Ulva became more friendly toward him. She also tried to learn his language. They used "sign language" to help them understand each other, and within a month could converse fairly easily.

Ulva explained that she was of the Tribe of Grask, one of the small marauding bands that had attacked the Clan and tried to steal their women. Grask was a cruel bully, who enjoyed hurting people and especially liked beating women. He had already killed two wives with his fists, and also one of the old men in their tribe who tried to protect his own wife from Grask's bullying.

Ulva had been another man's woman until last month, when Grask decided he wanted her. Ulva's man was young and much smaller than Grask, and rather than see him killed Ulva had willingly submitted to Grask's demands. He'd treated her reasonably well for the first few days, beating her only once when the water pitcher was empty. She'd accepted that, even though the pitcher leaked and she'd already filled it twice that day. But the next morning, Grask had awakened with pains in his head and blaming Ulva for them, beat her senseless. After that, he had beaten her daily for no good reason until she was so bruised, and so weak, she couldn't walk and had to crawl to the river for water. But Grask wasn't satisfied even then. He walked alongside her, jeering at her, kicking her when she didn't crawl fast enough.

And when he grew tired of that, he threw rocks at her. That's when Ulva decided something that before she would have never thought she was capable of even thinking: she decided to escape.

She waited until Grask fell asleep one night, then hit him on the head with one of his own rocks. She then left the tent, unnoticed, and limped off into the darkness. She kept moving throughout the night and pre-dawn, knowing that Grask would come after her the instant he regained consciousness, and finally made it to the river. She was hiding in the reeds, resting, when Moog and the other hunter's arrows drove her from cover.

Moog listened quietly while Ulva told him her story. By now, he had grown attached to her and knew he would kill to keep her. But there were Clan laws to abide by, and one of them was that no man could keep another hunter's wife if the latter wanted her back. Moog wasn't sure if that included wives from other clans, but knew, even if it did, he wasn't prepared to obey any laws that forced him to give up Ulva. Especially not to a bully like Grask. And sooner or later, Moog realized, Grask would track Ulva down and either try to take her by force or confront

Sangur and demand his wife be returned. Moog didn't think his own brother would force Moog to give up Ulva, but what if he did? Or what if the rest of the Clan insisted Ulva be turned over to Grask? What would Moog do then? Fight the very people who had been kind to him, and to Ulva?

It was a dilemma, and Moog struggled mightily with it. Day after day, when he wasn't hunting, he sat on the riverbank and tried to think of a better alternative than leaving the Clan and taking Ulva with him.

Then, one spring afternoon while he sat on the grassy bank by the rain-swollen, swift-moving river, watching Ulva splashing happily in the shallows, the dilemma was solved for him: Grask and his men jumped them.

Moog saw them coming. He sprang to his feet, bow and arrows in hand, and yelled for Ulva to run back to camp. But she wouldn't desert him. Instead, she joined him behind some rocks and held his arrows for him, so he could shoot them faster at Grask and his spear-throwing band. The arrows killed two men, and kept the others pinned down behind cover. But Moog, accurate as he was, knew his arrows would run out before he killed all of Grask's men. And then...?

"Can you swim?" he asked Ulva. He "signed" along with his words, so she wouldn't misunderstand him. She shook her head, no. "Then, hang onto me," Moog said. And shooting the last two arrows at Grask, who was inching closer, Moog grabbed Ulva's hand and together they plunged into the cold, swirling river.

Once they were in deep water, the swift-moving current pulled them under and they were swept along, clutched to each other, each holding their breath until they could break surface and gulp lungfuls of air. They were carried swiftly on downriver, Ulva clinging to Moog's neck while he desperately tried to keep afloat.

Grask and his men kept abreast of them, running along the riverbank and hurling spears at Moog. None hit him. And after a hundred yards or so, he and Ulva managed to hang onto a piece of driftwood that floated past. Kicking his powerful legs, Moog kept the driftwood in the middle of the river and out of range of the spears of Grask and his men.

They floated this way, swept along by the current, for over a mile. Then large, jagged rocks appeared in the river and the water turned white and foaming as it swirled around them, buffeting Moog and Ulva and threatening to tear them away from the driftwood.

By now Grask and his band had been out-distanced. But Moog and Ulva, not wanting to take chances, continued to hang onto the driftwood as it swirled them along through the raging white water.

The rapids lasted for almost a mile. Then, suddenly the rocks were gone and the water became calm. Moog and Ulva, exhausted, guided the driftwood into shore. There, they threw themselves onto a grassy bank and rested until their strength returned. They had no idea where they were, for no one in the Clan of Sangur had explored this far south, but they did know they couldn't go back. Somewhere behind them was Grask and his savage band, and Moog and Ulva knew that to try to return to camp was risking their lives. And though to continue on, alone, wasn't much safer, both felt it was better to face the unknown than the certainty of being killed by Grask.

When they were rested, Moog and Ulva ate berries and nuts that they picked from nearby bushes. Then, since there was still daylight, Moog decided they should continue downriver, putting as much distance as possible between themselves and Grask before they made camp. The river seemed the quickest way to travel, but Ulva, afraid of drowning, didn't want to return to the water. Moog was not that keen about being in the water, himself. So, he thought for awhile, then used a scraper-stone to hollow out part of the trunk of the lightning-struck hunk of tree. The water had softened the wood, and termites had already eaten away much of the rotted center, so Moog's task wasn't that hard. When he was finished, there was room for both of them to sit inside with their knees drawn-up, and still be able to paddle and steer with their hands.

Grateful and impressed by Moog's ingenuity, Ulva affectionately rubbed cheeks with her man before climbing aboard. Moog then pushed the driftwood boat into the water, jumped in and together they started paddling downriver.

The river went on for several miles before finally emptying into a large heart-shaped lake. Woods surrounded the lake. Moog and Ulva paddled ashore, made a crude shelter out of branches and leaves, crawled inside and fell asleep. They heard wild animals snuffling around the shelter during the night, but otherwise remained undisturbed. At dawn the next morning, Moog made a bow out of a mulberry branch, arrows out of reeds, and a bowstring from the sinew he always kept in his loin-pouch. The wood was strong and resilient and Moog knew it was ideal for bows. When he had time he would back it with strips of sinew, making it even more resilient. But for now he was satisfied and without going too far from the shelter, he quickly killed two birds. Ulva cooked the birds over a fire and they ate them for breakfast. "This would be a fine place to stay," she said, signing as she spoke. "There is plenty of game, and our young would grow strong and healthy in such peaceful surroundings."

Moog liked the area, but felt they still hadn't put enough distance between themselves and Grask. He wasn't sure just how far that "distance" needed to be, but it had to be farther than this for him to feel secure enough to settle down and raise a family.

Boarding their driftwood boat, they paddled around the lake and discovered a narrow waterway on the opposite shore. It wound south between woods and open grassland, through a steep-walled gorge, then seemingly ended at a big waterfall. The current pulled them through the cascading water, into a dark tunnel in the cliff that opened out into a small lake sheltered by high, smoke-blackened canyon walls. Charred trees and burnt stumps grew back from the water's edge and in among the trees, on the ash-whitened earth, were the burned-out remains of a village of tents. The smell of smoke permeated the windless air. And as Moog and Ulva paddled closer, they saw numerous canoes, some burned, others not, pulled up on the shore. They had never seen a canoe before, or anything like it, and were intrigued by its birch-bark-over-wooden-frame construction. They were also uneasy about what kind of greeting they would get from the men, women and children that emerged from the trees and lined the bank before them. Moog nocked an arrow and prepared to shoot the first hunter who raised his spear.

But the people, some of whom wore eagle feathers in their hair, showed no animosity. And when the children waded out into the shallows to help pull the driftwood boat ashore, Moog and Ulva knew they were among friends.

Neither Moog nor Ulva could understand the language these tall, proud, coppery-skinned people spoke, but they could "sign talk" to each other and soon learned that the Tribe of Kulak was preparing to leave the canyon and settle in an area that wasn't constantly devastated by fires caused by the lightning god. They also wanted to hunt where there were great herds of animals, like bison and mammoth, because their hunters still used spear-throwers and weren't as effective downing lone animals from long range.

Moog offered to teach the Kulaks how to make and shoot bows and arrows. He then demonstrated how well he could shoot to show the advantages of the weapon. Impressed, the tribe leader, Kulak the Elder, invited Moog and Ulva to accompany them. They happily agreed. Now, for the first time since leaving the Clan of Sangur, Moog and Ulva felt safe from an attack by Grask and his savages.

That afternoon, Moog, Ulva and the Tribe of Kulak paddled their canoes through the waterfall, out of the canyon, and back along the river for several hundreds yards until they reached a tributary that forked southeast. Kulak and his hunters had traveled this waterway many times, but never right to the end.

Now, singing to make their paddling easier, they followed its course for several miles. Then, as it grew dark, they beached their canoes on a grassy bank and made camp for the night.

Ulva helped the other women cook the evening meal while Moog and the men swapped hunting stories. It was a time for tall tales. Everyone enjoyed themselves and went to sleep in eager anticipation of tomorrow's journey.

What no one realized, however, was that this journey would carry them downriver across an invisible line that one day, in the distant future, would be known as the border between Canada and the United States.

Nor did these people, the Tribe of Kulak, realize they would become the first human beings to enter America. . .and that their ancestors would be known as Red Indians.

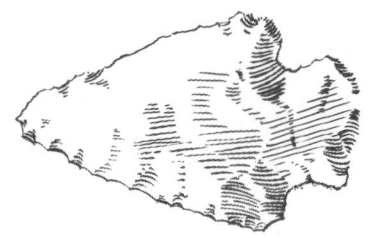

18,000 years ago, glaciers lowered worldwide sea levels to create land bridges and expand shorelines that narrowed the watery distances between numerous different countries. This enabled Cro-Magnon man to migrate to places that previously may have been impossible or too dangerous to reach...

One such watery distance affected by the lower sea levels was the Timor Straits, separating Australia from Southeast Asia. Subsiding waters linked Java, Sumatra and Borneo, and undoubtedly exposed many tiny islands to make "island-hopping" possible for Cro-Magnon man.

THE ABORIGINES

THE DEATH OF Nupo's older brother, Duni, had to be revenged. Worelu tribal laws dictated it. Their enemies, the Diburek, knew that when they killed him and Worelu knew it when they saw their spears in his body.

His corpse was found sprawled on the rocks beside the river. That was early this morning, and already the war drums were sounding and the Worelu were gathered about Duni's funeral pyre, mourning his death.

Tomorrow, the two tribes would meet on the usual battlefield, the Kalashi Plain, where they had settled their disputes by combat for as long as anyone could remember: because war between the Worelu and the Diburek was eternal. It was as expected as mosquitoes in summer; as essential as the rain that kept the jungles green and the rivers full. Without war none of the tribes that lived in the mountains and jungles of the island would feel any corporate identity. War gave everyone a powerful sense of unity; of togetherness. That is why the Worelu, and all their neighbors, perpetuated it by constantly killing one another...knowing, even as they did, that each death must be revenged.

Nor had anyone ever questioned this. No one, that is, until Nupo suggested to the Council Elders that it would be better not to retaliate, but to move away and find a place where they could live without war, without endless killing, and without practicing the final act of vengeance...the eating of their enemies' bodies.

The Elders became enraged. There had always been war and would always be war and anyone who suggested otherwise was a *kepu*, which was the worst form of coward, and should be branded an outcast. Nupo didn't want to be an outcast, for it meant that he could never marry or live in the village, or even wear a penis sheath, which was the right of every male from childhood on. So, from then on he kept his opinions to himself. And, like the rest of the tribe, went on warring and killing and eating the corpses of their enemies.

But he was not comfortable doing any of these things and finally, this morning, when the hunting party found his brother speared to death, he controlled his grief and vowed to himself that this would be the last time he would ever go to war or kill anyone again.

The next day, after a heavy rain and with the sky still hidden by black clouds, the battle between the two tribes went according to the accepted rules of combat. First, both sides gathered on the Kalashi Plain, fifty paces apart, and hurled challenges and insults at one another. Then, because it was Nupo's brother who had been killed, he was elected to lead the Worelu in a charge against the Diburek.

There were no trees or bushes on the plain, the constant battles held there over the ages having trampled everything flat. So the Worelu and the Diburek gathered on opposite sides of the plain, and, after dancing themselves into a frenzy, charged each other. Shouting war cries, the warriors ran doubled-over to protect their vulnerable body parts from the enemies' spears and arrows.

When they were close, Nupo obeyed the rules of combat by shooting the first arrow. Nocking one of his featherless reed shafts, with its inserted hardwood point, on his twisted fiber bowstring, he aimed at the nearest Diburek warrior. His laurel wood bow was four feet long and powerful enough to shoot an arrow sixty paces. But not accurately— which was why they had to get close to their enemies, or prey, before they shot. In his excitement, Nupo hurried his shot and the arrow missed its target. The Diburek howled with laughter and hurled more insults at the Worelu. Embarrassed, Nupo grabbed another arrow from the bunch held in his bowhand. Meanwhile, the battle had begun all around him. Both sides launched arrows and spears at each other. No one was hit in that opening attack, and the battle continued until finally each tribe had incurred several casualties. Then all the warriors retired temporarily, and allowed the old men to tend to the wounded.

Dark clouds were forming overhead, and both tribes anxiously wondered if the rain god, Aku, would order them to stop fighting. But after a short wait, when there was no rain, the warriors on both sides reformed their battle lines and, screaming war cries, attacked each other once more.

Nupo again led the charge and this time, saw his second arrow hit one of the Diburek warriors facing him. He was only a boy, no more than twelve, and as Nupo's arrow sank into his chest he went down with an agonized scream. Nupo watched him, wondering why he didn't feel elated by the death of an enemy. The boy was naked save for his neck beads and the two-foot-long reed sheathing his penis. Hands clutching his wound, he writhed in agony on the ground. A strange feeling Nupo didn't understand stirred inside him—a feeling that made him want to help the boy—and he started toward him. But warriors on either side of him reached the boy first, and stabbed him to death with their long, hardwood-pointed spears.

Diburek warriors sprang toward the Worelu, hurling their spears as they charged. One of Nupo's tribe went down, pierced through the heart, and as other Diburek warriors closed in, the Worelu quickly fell back. Nupo felt an arrow graze his shoulder, bringing a searing pain. But before he could turn and see how close his pursuers were, it suddenly thundered and within moments started to rain.

All fighting stopped. The warriors had somehow displeased the rain god and the battle was over. Both tribes collected their wounded and carried them back to their villages.

It was night when the Worelu reached the collection of small round thatched huts built on a hilltop clearing, and one of the wounded was dying. He was taken to the Man-Who-Heals' hut and placed on a bed of palm fronds. The Man-Who-Heals made small cuts in the warrior's stomach to release the "evil blood", then crouched over him waving a fetish to chase away enemy spirits. It was a powerful fetish, made from a stick of sugar cane with the feathers of many sacred birds bound to it, but the god of war loved this warrior and nothing could be done to keep his spirit on earth.

Outside the Man-Who-Heals' hut a funeral pyre was built and Nupo and the others gathered around it to watch the warrior's corpse burn and the smoke to carry his spirit up to the god of war. But instead of the smoke curling upward, it blew toward Nupo, covering him so that he couldn't see or breathe without choking. He jumped backward, coughing and wiping his eyes. Immediately everyone shouted that the slain warrior's spirit had accused him of causing the warrior's death! Nupo tried to argue, but he was still coughing from the smoke and couldn't get out any words. The Council Elders recalled what Nupo shad aid about stopping war and killing, and ordered the men to beat the spirit of life out of him. He protest loudly, but it was useless. Through his stinging, watery eyes Nupo saw the men grab their clubs and close in on him. He ran from the village, chased by men who, moments before, had been his friends and who were now intent on killing him. His only hope of survival was to out-distance them. He ran downhill as fast as he could, barely feeling the dirt or loose stones underfoot, and reached the forest at the base of the hill ahead of his pursuers. He raced into the trees, squinting to see in the darkness as he stumbled over bushes and roots in his path. He knew the jungle well. But so did his pursuers, and many of them could outrun him. Already, in fact, a few were closing in on him...

Frightened, Nupo wearily headed east into Iboku territory,

hoping the men chasing him wouldn't dare risk an encounter with the island's most dreaded tribe. It was a gamble with death, because the clubs of his pursuers would kill him much faster than the slow-burning torture fires of the Iboku. But anything was better than immediate, certain death. And as he ran on, heart pounding in his chest, Nupo told himself that this way, there was at least a chance he might be able to slip through Iboku territory undetected.

He guessed correctly. Nupo's pursuers stopped following him as soon as they realized they were entering Iboku country. He ran on, slower now and with more caution, hoping that he wouldn't stumble into any Iboku outposts. His chances of surviving were better if he keep to the forest, since the Iboku, like all the other tribes, built their villages in clearings and posted sentries atop tall wooden watch-towers to prevent raiding parties from surprising them.

Afraid to stop or rest, Nupo kept moving all night. He passed two Iboku villages without being detected, and by dawn he had reached the end of their territory and could smell salt in the cool breeze blowing through the trees. Ahead, beyond the trees, the plain sloped steeply down to the ocean. Nupo hurried on, and when he was out of the trees he saw the swamp forest far below and, beyond, the trees thinning out as they grew in the brackish tidal swamp. Nupo had never been here before, but he'd heard the Elders speak of the great ocean of salt water that surrounded them, and he felt himself trembling as he shaded his eyes against the rising sun and looked beyond the trees at the endless expanse of gray-blue water.

Here and there tiny coral islands and reefs poked up through the ocean, almost like stepping stones. Worelu tribal legends said that their ancestors came from other islands similar to these; and that in the beginning, when an era called the "Last Age of Ice" allowed their forefathers to walk where there was now water, all humans were born of the same mother. If that was true, Nupo thought, perhaps that was why he didn't want to kill men who were no less than his distant brothers.

But it was all a great puzzlement to him; a puzzle everyone

was too fearful to talk about—even the Council Elders—so he was left with only a lot of unanswered questions...

Now, as he squinted in the bright early light, Nupo could see a far-off, hazy outline on the horizon that he guessed was a large island.

He wondered what kind of people lived there, and if they would kill him or call him an outcast if he tried to join them. It didn't really matter, anyway, he told himself, because it was too far to swim and too dangerous to try to cross in a river dugout.

Nupo climbed down the steep slope to the beginning of the swamp. Swarms of mosquitoes attacked him. And as he waded through the murky, waist-deep water, brilliantly plumed birds flew, squawking, out of hidden nests and he heard small animals plunging off through the undergrowth.

Now and then frightened snakes swam past, only their heads above water as they tried to wriggle out of his way. He waded on, keeping to the shallows and climbing over the huge, partly submerged roots of great trees whose lofty, interwoven branches formed a leafy green ceiling that shut out all but a few rays of sunlight.

After Nupo had followed the coastal waters for several miles, he found a strange raft wedged between two trees. The raft was made of bundles of bark lashed together by twisted fibers. It was manmade, yet there were no warriors around and he realized the raft must have floated there, unattended. Tired of wading, Nupo climbed aboard the raft and used a broken branch to paddle it along the endless waterways.

Finally, he reached the mouth of a wide river. The strong current surprised him and he was swept seaward. Before he could paddle inland again, he was caught by several large rolling waves that threatened to capsize the raft. And when he tried to paddle, the force of the waves breaking jerked the branch from his hands. Fearful, Nupo lay on his stomach and clung to the fiber holding the raft together. He also prayed to the great god of the oceans not to snatch his spirit from his body. He had only lived for twenty rainy seasons and wanted very much to enjoy his remaining years. Spray showered over him, the salt stinging his eyes. He closed his eyes and just hung on, feeling the raft being pitched about by the turbulent waves...

For a long time he rode the waves this way. Then, finally, after what seemed like hours, the waves lessened and he found myself floating calmly. He opened his eyes. To his dismay, he saw he was a great distance from the shore and had nothing with which to steer or paddle the raft. But at least he was still alive, and he thanked the Great Salt Water god for answering his prayers.

He drifted aboard the raft for several hours, the current always pulling him toward the distant shoreline that he'd seen earlier from the hilltop. Occasionally, huge turtles swam past the raft. They were many times larger than the river turtles that the Worelu hunted, and Nupo was fearful that a collision with one of them would sink his raft.

Ahead, he could see land quite clearly now and realized it wasn't an island or an atoll, but a coastline that stretched for as far as he could see. He grew fearful. What kind of people and dangers would he meet when he got there?

As he got closer, he saw a large headland with craggy sandstone cliffs that eons of offshore winds had whittled into odd shapes.

Below the cliffs were narrow sandy beaches. The waves broke on the beaches and Nupo rode one in, lying on his stomach while clinging to the raft and hoping he wouldn't be thrown off onto the sharp coral that he could see just below the surface.

He was lucky. The wave he rode carried the raft up the beach and deposited it calmly, almost gently, on the sand. He jumped off, his legs a little unsteady, and anxiously looked around. The beach was empty but on the cliff above him, he saw several warriors watching him. They were tall, gaunt men, completely naked, and their blackish skin was burned leathery by the sun. Their hair was long and unruly, black where not sun-bleached, and they wore no feathers or head decoration. Shockingly, nor did they wear penis sheaths! Nor bones or ornaments through their ears or noses. Nupo realized they must be very primitive, and wondered what other differences he would discover about them. Their only weapon was a long stone-pointed spear, held at the rear by a wooden throwing stick. They showed no signs of aggression and Nupo sensed they were more curious than hostile.

He held up his hands, palms facing the warriors, to show he was unarmed. For a few moments, they whispered among each other. Then, satisfied that he was not dangerous, they climbed down from the rocky cliffs and joined Nupo on the beach. They spoke to him in a language he didn't understand, but their gestures indicated they wanted to know where he had come from. Nupo pointed out to sea, and tried to explain about his own island. They did not understand his words, but managed to get the gist of what he was saying and nodded and laughed and excitedly clapped their hands. Then they led him along the beach, around some rocks, to where several women and children were gathered about a driftwood fire. The naked women, who were as gaunt as the men, were cooking fish on pointed sticks over the flames until the flesh blackened. They then removed the fish from the stick, quickly so that they did not get burned, and shared it among the children.

Everyone stared at Nupo as he approached with the warriors, especially the children. But again, he sensed no aggression, just curiosity, and he began to relax and lose the fear that they were going to kill him and eat him.

The warriors discussed Nupo with the women. By their looks, gestures and pointing out to sea he guessed they were explaining where he came from. The women seem unconcerned, as if his arrival wasn't that unusual an event, and Nupo wondered if over the years these people, and others, had arrived here the same way. The children were even more curious, and continued staring and talking about him among themselves long after the adults had lost interest in him.

Once Nupo was accepted, one of the women gave him a cooked fish. He realized he hadn't eaten since early yesterday; and after a nod of thanks, wolfed the fish down. It was hot enough to burn the mouth, but tasted crispy and delicious. He swallowed all but the biggest bones, and when he was finished eating he was given a gourd of water to drink. He drank it all in one long gulp. He then asked the warriors where their camp was, but they didn't understand him.

When the meal was over, the women and children collected their belongings and followed the warriors up a steep path that climbed to the clifftops. They gestured for Nupo to accompany them. He did, despite his weariness, and when they reached the top of the cliffs he saw they were in brush country The land was dotted with tall trees with peeling bark and long, thin, silvery-green leaves that had a pungent odor about them. Nupo had never seen them before and at a later time, when he'd learned some of the language, heard the trees called eucalyptus.

That night they stopped near some rocks, lit another fire and made preparations to sleep. It dawned on Nupo that these nomads probably had no permanent camp but merely wandered about, without a territory of their own to guard, or an enemy's border to fight over. He was amazed. And at the same time, relieved. This meant less warring and killing—something he had always wanted but knew would never happen among the tribes on his island.

But he found it strange that people would not make a permanent camp. It took away any feeling of solidarity or unity, replacing it with a rootlessness that he found unsettling. No doubt he would grow used to it, though. For these were friendly people and good hunters and trackers, who with the aid of the throwing stick could throw a spear very accurately and for a greater distance than Nupo had believed possible.

He guessed this was why they had never bothered to make bows and arrows; that and the fact that the local trees bent with little resistance and would not hurl an arrow with the kind of force needed to kill wild game.

Understanding this, Nupo saw no need to mention bows and arrow.

Instead, in the weeks ahead, as everyone kept moving in search of food and water, he practiced using the spear thrower until he could hurl a spear as far and as accurately as any warrior in the tribe.

Several months passed. Nupo could now speak many words of his new language, and had proved himself a fine provider. Everyone was pleased that he had joined the tribe. Especially Trugeena, a young girl as slim as a spear who has a quick, pleasing laugh, bright dark eyes and a beautiful broad flat nose and big teeth. Nupo liked Trugeena, and knew she liked him. One day soon he intended to ask her father to sell her to him. If he agreed, and the two men could reach a fair price, Nupo planned to marry Trugeena. Then, she could cook for him, bear his children. . .and be his constant companion as they wandered about this harsh but seemingly peaceful land.

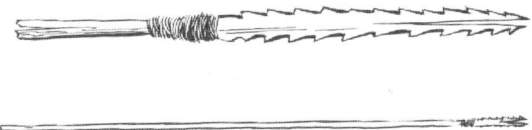

The Mummy of Ramses II was found in a shaft at Der-el-Bahri in 1881. With it were the mummies of two other Pharoahs, Ramses I and Seti I. According to ancient records inscribed on the royal coffins the mummies had been transferred from several previous, grander and more fitting tombs in the Valley of the Kings to avoid further vandalism by grave-robbers.

All the enormous wealth that was originally buried with the Pharoahs had been plundered long ago, but among the few remaining royal possessions of Rameses 11 was a triangular bow of Hittite or Assyrian origin. Since the Pharoah was in his nineties when he died, he would have been too frail to pull the powerful war bow, so why was it special enough to be buried alongside him?

THE EGYPTIANS

IN 1288 B.C., after the spring rains had stopped, Ramses II led his army northward along the coast of Phoenicia, then marched inland up the valley of the Dog River.

It was a large army by Egyptian standards, over twenty thousand men, many of which were Nubian and Sherden mercenaries. The army was divided into four divisions, each named after one of the great gods: Amon, Re, Ptah and Sutekh. Ramses commanded the Amon Division, amongst which was an elite corps of Nubian foot-archers from the Mazoi tribe. Well-disciplined and fearless, the muscular black-skinned warriors used self-wood, recurve bows and arrows made of reeds with bronze points. The young Pharoah admired the courage and skill of these bowmen, and along with his Sherden chariot archers, who used long-range composite bows, assigned them to be part of his household guard.

Ramses' campaign against the Hittites had begun several years ago when the Hittite king, Metella, had gathered a large army and captured the strategically positioned city of Kadesh, the center of Syrian power in the days of Thutmose III, Ramses' great ancestor. Knowing that his father, Seti I, had not been able to dislodge the Hittites from Syria, Ramses II first gained control of the harbors along the Phoenician coast so that he would have easy access to Egypt by water. Then, aware that his presence must now be known to King Metella, Ramses marched toward Syria. He left behind one of his most-trusted commanders, with orders to conscript as many new recruits into the army as he could find...and to then follow him.

The terrain inland was made up of steep rocky hills that the army found difficult to cross. After three weeks' of slow-going under a boiling sun, Ramses, impatient to do battle, ordered the leaders of the other divisions to follow as fast as they could, then force-marched his own division into the precipitous valley of the Orontes River.

It was a strenuous march through hot, high-walled canyons and over uneven, rock-strewn scrubland, with men and horses suffering from the heat, dust and innumerable insect bites. But urged on by the energetic Pharoah, the troops wearily pushed themselves to the limit and on the twenty ninth day, they reached the heights overlooking the vast plain that lay before the city of Kadesh.

Now, only a day's march from his enemy, Ramses let his weary soldiers rest while scouts were sent out to try to locate where the Hittite army was camped. While awaiting their return, the Pharoah, a tall, slender, impetuous man in his late twenties, looked back across the hills to the south in hopes of seeing signs of his other divisions. But Re, Ptah and Sutekh straggled too far behind to be seen with the naked eye, and Ramses, angered by their slowness, sent riders to urge the divisions to join him as swiftly as they could.

At dawn his scouts returned to say they had found no sign of the enemy, anywhere. Believing that the Hittite army had taken refuge inside Kadesh's strong walls, an encouraged Ramses struck camp and led his troops down the steep slope that descended to the River Orontes. Here, near Shabtuna, a town the

Hebrews later renamed Riblah, the river emerged from the sheer-sided, gorgelike valley through which it had previously flowed, and ran curving across the great plain to Kadesh, and beyond.

Ramses halted his troops on the banks of the river. There, dismounting from his chariot, he and his commanders inspected the river and found it suitable to ford. Kadesh being located on the west side of the river, Ramses ordered the Division of Amon across. The foot soldiers were slow in assembling, and word reached the Pharoah that they and some of his charioteers were reluctant to go any farther without the support of the other three divisions.

Angered by their cowardice, Ramses climbed into his chariot and ordered his driver to start across the river. Shamed, the other chariots followed immediately. Encouraged by the sight of more than a thousand chariots churning across the river, the rest of the division joined ranks and marched into the cold, waist-high water.

Once everyone was across, Ramses sent his scouts ahead to locate the Hittite encampment. They returned shortly with two local Bedouins, who claimed to be deserters from King Metella's army. They bore recent whip-marks across their backs, and eagerly assured Ramses that the Hittite army had retreated as soon as they heard of the Pharoah's approach and were now camped to the north near Aleppo. Since his scouts hadn't seen any sign of the enemy elsewhere, Ramses believed the Bedouins and quickly gave orders to march. His commanders, alarmed by the inadequacy of their puny force, begged the Pharoah to wait until the rest of his divisions caught up with them. But Ramses ignored their advice and impetuously pressed on, hoping to reach Kadesh and to start besieging the city that same day.

His fast, light chariots soon out-distanced the infantry and by late morning Ramses, accompanied by only his household guard, drew within sight of Kadesh.

The Egyptians were also within sight of King Metella's scouts, who were hidden among rocks near the river. Realizing Ramses must have believed the two treacherous Bedouin spies, who had been well-paid for their lies and the mild whipping, the scouts withdrew and rode back to the Hittite camp located just northwest of Kadesh.

Metella, a short, powerfully built man with fierce dark eyes, a sharp nose and thick black hair hanging to his shoulders, sat in the shade of his tent and listened as his scouts reported what they had seen. The king was delighted that he had tricked Ramses. Like all Hittites, he feared and hated the Egyptians for their arrogant, conquering ways. A year ago, when he'd learned that the Pharoah's army had captured the ports along the Phoenician coast and was marching toward Syria, Metella had ordered all the vassal kings of his vast empire to supply him with soldiers. The kings, all ancient enemies of Egypt, had willingly complied. But Metella, feeling his force still wasn't large enough to defeat Ramses, opened his royal coffers and paid mercenaries to join him.

Wild Lycian pirates, Cilicians, Mysians and Dardanians—all swelled the ranks of the Hittite army. Finally satisfied by the size of his force, Metella made elaborate plans to outwit the Egyptians, then marched out to engage the proud young Pharoah's soldiers.

Now, as he sat in the cool shade of his Imperial tent, the wily Hittite king gave orders to his commanders to move the army to the east side of the river. Almost thirty thousand men, in chariots and on foot, quickly crossed the River Orontes. As they moved, they made sure they kept the city of Kadesh between themselves and the advancing Egyptians. They then took up positions behind Ramses and his household guard, cutting off their retreat.

If Metella had attacked Ramses then, in force, it would have been all over for the young Pharoah. His household guard, though well-trained and devotedly loyal, were too few to have withstood even one charge by the massive Hittite army—which included two thousand five hundred war chariots. But Metella, wary of prior Egyptian military ploys, wanted to make certain he himself wasn't being led into a trap; so he sent out scouts to verify that the Pharoah was indeed separated from his main force.

Ramses, meanwhile, unaware of the impending danger, pitched camp northwest of Kadesh and awaited the arrival of the

Division of Amon. The weary soldiers arrived within the hour and camped protectively around their leader's royal tent. It was early afternoon now and gradually the supply trains plodded in. The oxen were unyoked and the wagons added to the barricade of shields already encircling the camp.

In the shade of his tent Ramses ate sparingly, then called in his commanders and made plans for attacking the city. The Egyptian forces were presently split into three groups: Ramses and the Amon Division were northwest of Kadesh; the Division of Re was en route just the south of the city; and the Divisions of Ptah and Sutekh had not yet even forded the River Orontes below Shabtuna.

The Egyptian commanders wisely wanted to wait until all the divisions had joined them before launching any attack upon Kadesh. Ramses, typically, wanted to attack the city at once. After all, he was a devine being, a god, and gods waited for no man. His officers respected his exulted status, bowed to it in fact, but gently reminded the young ruler that they and his soldiers were not gods, just mere mortals, and if they were going to die for their Pharoah (which they would gladly do), they wanted it to be in a winning cause. And that meant waiting until they were joined by the rest of their forces.

Before Ramses could protest, guards entered the tent with a Hittite scout. He'd been captured not far from the encampment, and when beaten had confessed that King Metella and his army were concealed, ready to strike, just south of the Egyptian position.

Shocked and angered by the alarming news, Ramses berated his commanders for failing to report that the enemy was dangerously close. The young Pharoah then dispatched messengers to ride to the Divisions of Ptah and Sutekh and order them to join him as swiftly as possible. Another rider was sent to find the Division of Re, which Ramses believed was only a few miles from his camp, and to warn them of the closeness of the Hittite army.

But as the messenger rode from the camp, he was confronted by an appalling sight: less than one third of the soldiers of the Re Division, most of which were badly wounded, came running across the plain toward him! They were in full flight, a disorganized mass of beaten men fleeing from the Hittite chariots that had suddenly ridden down on them from the river. In the distance, the rider could see about a hundred of these chariots chasing the routed Egyptians. Without waiting to see where the rest of the Hittite army was, he galloped back to camp and alerted the Pharoah.

Stunned, Ramses rushed his infantry out onto the plain to halt the Hittite attack. Massed in a close phalanx formation, with the foot bowmen on both flanks, the Egyptians calmly waited for the oncoming chariots.

Hittite chariots were bigger and stronger than the Egyptian chariots, for they carried an extra man—a shield bearer whose job was to protect the archer. This left the driver unprotected except for his light, scale armor. Aware of this, the archers waited until the chariots were within arrow range, then concentrated on the drivers.

The bronze-pointed arrows penetrated the Hittite armor, and driver after driver was killed, leaving their chariots unguided. Many overturned, others collided with each other, the rest plunged headlong into the Egyptian phalanx.

The first three ranks of the phalanx caved-in under the weight of the charging horses, but the rest held firm. Swords swinging, spears thrusting, the soldiers closed in and dragged the Hittites from their chariots. The battle was short and bloody. In twenty minutes the Egyptian infantry had killed every Hittite. But their own losses had been heavy, and Ramses watched in dismay as he saw the number of wounded among the soldiers limping back into camp.

Calling the few remaining officers of the Re Division into his royal tent, the young Pharoah angrily demanded an explanation for their defeat and the loss of over half a division. Stumbling over the words, the still-dazed and dejected commanders explained that the division had been marching across the plain toward Kadesh when, without warning, the entire Hittite chariotry had charged down on them. Caught completely off-guard, the division had tried to rally but it was hopeless. The more than two thousand chariots swept right through them, literally cutting them to pieces! The few panicked survivors had either fled south to join the Divisions of Ptah and Sutekh, or, like themselves, raced north to join Ramses and the Amon Division.

Ramses, realizing that King Metella had out-maneuvered him, summoned the commanders of the Amon Division to plan a counter-attack. But before the Pharoah could outline his plans, a scout rushed in, prostrated himself before Ramses and begged for permission to speak. Given it, the scout blurted out that to the south and east all the Hittite chariots were massing for a full-scale attack...while less than a mile away King Metella was about to ford the river with eight thousand of his finest infantry.

The commanders panicked. Heavily out-numbered and in their weakened condition, the division's only hope of survival was to fall back and they begged Ramses to give the order immediately.

The Pharoah refused, berated them for their cowardice and hurried outside. There, he mustered his elite household guard, climbed into his chariot and boldly charged his small force at the Hittite chariots lined along the eastern bank of the river.

The unexpected attack surprised the Hittites, but by sheer weight of numbers they forced Ramses' mercenaries to withdraw. The Hittites cheered, and banged his spears against their shields. But victory was not theirs. Regrouping, Ramses led his warriors on a second desperate charge that broke through the Hittite line and drove them back to the river. With the enemy scattered and fleeing, Ramses again wisely withdrew to regroup and evaluate the situation.

It didn't look good. Charging across the open plain to his south was the main force of Hittite chariotry; while across the river King Metella's infantry were preparing to come to the aid of their defeated comrades. Ramses knew in a very short time his meager army would be trapped and crushed between two overwhelming forces. The fate of Egypt seemed doomed.

Then, remembering the greed of the Hittites, Ramses had an idea. Galloping back to camp, he ordered his commanders to muster every soldier, including the wounded, and to join him at the river. And take nothing with you," he commanded as his servants and the servants of the high-ranking officers prepared to dismantle the tents and gather up their personal belongings.

"Leave everything in plain sight for the enemy. Especially the casks of wine!"

His officers angrily protested, for the army had reaped ample plunder from its many victories since leaving Egypt. But Ramses was adamant, warning that anyone disobeying him would be killed.

He then left camp and rode back to his household guard, who awaited him on the long gradual slope facing the river. As his driver reined in the plunging horses at the crest of the slope, one of the Nubian captains approached Ramses' chariot, pointed westward and asked the young Pharoah if he could see something glinting on the horizon. Ramses shaded his eyes against the glare and tried to identify a strange glint on the western horizon. He knew instantly it was spear points reflecting the late afternoon sunlight. It couldn't be his two straggling divisions, Ptah and Sutekh, for they were to the south. Therefore, it had to be the enemy—more Hittites, hurrying to join King Metella and join in the slaughter of the hated Egyptians. Ramses now realized why Metella hadn't crossed the river with his infantry; he was waiting until his reinforcements arrived.

The young Egyptian's heart sank. But, not wanting to show his fear to his troops, the Pharoah dismissed the glint, saying it was only the sun shining on the rocks. Then, seeing that all the soldiers from the camp were now mustered on the slope with the household guard, Ramses drew his sword and bravely charged the Hittite chariots that were trying to regroup beside the river.

Across the river, King Metella stood in his big gilded war chariot at the head of his infantry and watched the Egyptians attacking his chariots. His impatient commanders begged the king to order the infantry across, so they could drive the Egyptians back into the main force of Hittite chariotry that could be seen advancing in two long lines across the plain. But Metella, unlike Ramses, was a very cautious, deliberate man who had waited too long to annihilate the Pharoah, and his army, to rush into any decision that might later prove to be a costly blunder. Better to wait, he thought as he watched the fierce fighting on the opposite riverbank, and lose some extra lives, than to strike too early and have the accursed Egyptians somehow escape from his trap.

So, Metella watched, unmoved by the unnecessary killing of his own soldiers by Egyptian swords, spears and arrows, waiting to see which way the tide of battle would turn before he committed his infantry.

Meanwhile, on the plain, the main force of the Hittite chariotry now reached the unprotected camp of the Egyptian forces. Suspecting a trap, the commanders halted outside the barricade and ordered a search party to check inside the tents. When they proved to be empty, the Hittites rushed into the deserted camp, jumped from their chariots and, as Ramses had anticipated, began plundering the Egyptian booty. At the river, the accuracy of Ramses' archers had begun to sway the battle in favor of the Egyptians. Standing in groups of four, shooting in well-disciplined unison, the Nubian foot bowmen took deadly toll of the Hittite chariot drivers. Man after man fell to earth, pierced by the Nubian arrows, leaving the driverless chariots to race madly in all directions. Taking advantage of the chaotic disorder, Ramses led his own chariots into the mass of struggling humanity, cutting the disorganized Hittites to pieces.

On the opposite riverbank, King Metella watched his soldiers being slaughtered in grim, silent rage. A cold, unsettling despair filled his soul. Would the wretched, indomitable Egyptians *never* be defeated?

Shortly, his commanders again begged him to give the order for the infantry to ford the river and join the battle. But once more Metella refused. As long as the infantry remained on this side of the river, the Egyptians could not cross and escape; and on the plain, once his greedy commanders stopped plundering the Egyptian camp, the mass of chariotry prevented Ramses' force from escaping to the south or west. All Metella had to do was have patience and wait: in due time, the Egyptians would crushed and total victory would be his.

But it was not to be. The "strange glint" in the west that Ramses' had identified earlier as enemy reinforcements, was now close enough to be recognized as an army of mercenaries,

Ramses bravely charged the Hittite chariots.

led by the Egyptian commander whom the Pharoah had left on the Phoenician coast to gather new recruits.

This army closed in on the unsuspecting Hittites plundering the Egyptian camp, and massacred every last man.

At the river, Ramses received word from a messenger about the arrival of the newly recruited army and, elated, quickly passed the news along to his fighting men. Greatly encouraged, the Egyptian soldiers attacked the remaining Hittite chariotry with renewed vigor. The Hittites broke ranks and fled, driving their chariots into the river. The Egyptians pursued them, and on the opposite bank King Metella watched in bitter dismay as many of his officers and men were slaughtered by the aroused Egyptians. The survivors reached the opposite riverbank and begged their king to march against the victorious Egyptians. But for a final time Metella refused; and instead marched downriver, forded at a shallow place opposite Kadesh, and took refuge inside the city's high walls.

Although victory was temporarily theirs, the Egyptian forces had suffered enormous losses—especially in the Division of Re, which had been almost completely wiped out. Ramses, depressed by the death of so many of his warriors and knowing that any attempt to oust the Hittites from Kadesh would result in untold slaughter on both sides, decided his campaign had already been successful enough to warrant returning to Egypt. And despite the arrival of the Division of Ptah that evening, and news that the Division of Sutekh was only a day's march behind them, the young Pharoah apprised his commanders of his decision: the offensive was over and they would start back to Egypt in the morning. Later, when Ramses was alone in his royal tent, the commander of the Nubian bowmen begged an audience with the Pharoah. Ramses permitted him to enter and after prostrating himself before his ruler, the Nubian rose and offered Ramses a memento of the battle at the river: a Hittite bow belonging to King Aleppo, one of the vassal kings who had commanded the Hittite chariotry.

Ramses smiled. The last time he had seen Aleppo, the king was being dragged out of the river by Hittite infantrymen, who then managed to revive the half-drowned king by unceremoniously holding him upside down and thumping the water out of him!

Thanking the Nubian commander, Ramses then dismissed him and placed the short, triangular bow at his bedside. It was small compensation when compared to the failure of capturing of a city as rich and strategic as Kadesh, but it was something the young Pharoah would keep among his most-treasured possessions for the rest of his life. . .and, after-life.

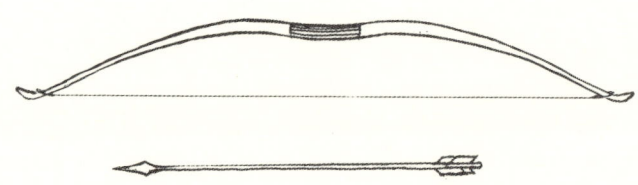

It is well-known that Alexander the Great was one of the greatest generals of all time, noted for his brilliant military strategy and for the rapidity with which he could cross great distances and crush his enemies.

What is not quite so well-known is the fact that Alexander may have been responsible for introducing the bow and arrow into western India.

THE MACEDONIANS

IN 326 B.C. Alexander, king of the Macedonians, sent half of his army through the Khyber Pass to the Indus, with instructions to cross the river and await his next orders. With the rest of his forces he advanced to Taxila, a large town located at the hub of the trade routes from Bactria, Kashmir, and the Ganges Valley.

There he met with the local rajah, Taxiles, who made Alexander a gift of seven hundred of his finest cavalry. His friendliness toward Alexander was prompted by the fact that he was at war with a neighboring rajah, a giant of a man called Porus, and needed the young Macedonian leader's help to defeat him.

Alexander, through his spies, knew the motive behind Taxiles' gift, but happily accepted the well-trained horsemen, anyway. His campaign to extend his empire into India had forced him to fight the local rulers throughout the Punjab, and his many victorious battles against the warlike tribes had depleted his forces.

Now, in spring, Alexander's scouts reported that Porus was

camped on the River Hydaspes with a large army, determined to repel the Macedonian invaders. Presently, the force under Alexander's command consisted of the Royal Squadron and four regiments of Companions, the Bactrian, Sogdian, and Scythian cavalry, one thousand mounted archers, two infantry battalions, the Guards, Agrianians and a contingent of foot-archers.

Alexander's spies estimated King Porus' forces were three times that number. The young Macedonian ruler, realizing he needed the rest of his army, dispatched word to his generals, Perdiccas and Hephaestion, who were still camped on the Indus, to dismantle the boats and transport them overland to the banks of the Hydaspes, where they could be reassembled. They were also to bring his slingers, siege-engines, and reserve supply of bows and arrows for his legions of archers.

Alexander then made Philip, the son of Machata, governor of all the territory between the Indus and the Hydaspes and left him in Taxila with a formidable garrison. Then, satisfied he would not be attacked from the rear, Alexander mustered his army and marched out to attack King Porus.

His first concern was to cross the Hedaspes. By now it was early summer and the river was swollen by torrential monsoon rains and melted snow from the mountains. His scouts also reported that Porus' forces were reinforced by two hundred elephants trained for battle. Alexander had encountered war elephants in previous campaigns against the rajahs. He knew his horses were terrified by the beasts' scent, which meant they would panic and jump off the rafts as they crossed the river. This necessitated crossing at a place undetected by the enemy—no easy task, for King Porus' was a cunning, fearless warrior and his patrols monitored Alexander's every move along the river. And at each suitable fording point, war elephants were rushed up to meet Alexander's forces.

Realizing he needed to outwit his adversary, the wily young Macedonian king made numerous fake attempts to cross the river, each time withdrawing just as Porus' war elephants arrived.

It took several weeks, under deplorable weather conditions, but the maneuver finally worked. The lumbering, festooned beasts, their howdahs bristling with weapons, gradually grew tired from the constant re-positioning. And Porus, fearing they would not be fit enough to repel the invaders' real attack, finally stopped sending the elephants, relying instead on his scouts to give him sufficient warning to call up his main force. Alexander was now ready to cross. He selected a narrow bend in the river near Jalalpur, twenty miles from his camp, across from a wooded island that would hide his crossing from Porus' scouts. As additional camouflage, Alexander left a large number of his forces in camp under Craterus' command. Their orders were to make preparations as if they intended to cross at this point, hopefully decoying Porus into deploying his main army to meet them.

Meanwhile, under cover of a violent thunderstorm, Alexander led the rest of his army across the river. It was a treacherous crossing, the swirling waters chest-high in most places, and many men were swept away by the current. But there was no panic. With Alexander were very capable and loyal commanders who would one day become kings: Ptolemy, Seleucus and Lysimachus. Under their able command, and with Hephaestion and Perdiccas beside them, the disciplined men and rafted horses finally reached the opposite bank of the river.

As the soldiers struggled ashore, they were spotted by Porus' scouts, who rode through the storm to alert their king. Not sure if this was just another feint by Alexander, or the real attack, Porus sent one of his sons with a column of chariots and two thousand cavalry to repel the invaders. It was too late. Alexander's main force was already ashore, and after a short, fierce battle they massacred all the Indian troops, including Porus' son.

When Porus heard of the defeat, he realized this was no bluff by Alexander. Momentarily putting aside his grief, the powerful rajah prepared to attack him.

But before the army was ready to march, the king received word from another scout that Craterus was threatening to cross the river with his force from the main camp. Confronted by this dilemma, King Porus showed good sense as a leader. Deploying a small force to keep Craterus at bay, he marched against Alexander with the rest of his army.

When Alexander sighted Porus' forces, they were already maneuvering into a favorable position. Seeing their superior numbers, Alexander halted and waited for his infantry to catch up. When they arrived, exhausted from marching through the mud and monsoon rains, he used good judgement and allowed them to rest while he planned his strategy.

Knowing that it was suicidal to advance head-on into Porus' war elephants, Alexander devised a battle plan that would make the beasts work for him: he sent his Thracian horse-archers to attack the left wing of Porus' cavalry. Then, once they were engaged in battle, he charged them with part of his own cavalry. The Indian right-wing cavalry galloped around to support the left wing. As soon as they did, Alexander sent the remainder of his cavalry to attack them from the rear. Caught between the Macedonian "pincers," Porus' cavalry fell back in panic, exposing both flanks of the long line of elephants.

Anticipating this, Alexander sent in his infantry. But the elephants were too much for them. The massive beasts trampled hundreds to death, causing great gaps in their lines. Spearmen in the howdahs atop the elephants' backs killed hundreds more and Alexander's infantry retreated in chaos. Seeing this, King Porus ordered the elephants to pursue the fleeing Macedonians and for awhile the outcome of the battle flowed in Porus' favor.

But Alexander again turned to his Thracian horse-archers, ordering them to shoot the mahouts on the elephants' backs. The horsemen made several sweeping attacks, showering the mahouts with arrows. Under this withering fire, all the mahouts were soon killed. Then, when the beasts had no drivers to control them, the archers shot the elephants themselves. Arrows sticking out all over them, the pain-maddened beasts went berserk and trampled their own men.

It was a cruel and gruesome sight. Dying elephants, trumpeting in rage and pain, flailed helplessly in the blood-stained mud. Others, still on their feet, madly gored each other as well as the soldiers fighting around them. Meanwhile, the relentless monsoon rains beat down on everyone. Finally, in a last-ditch effort to save themselves, Porus' men tried to cut a path through the ever-tightening ring of Macedonian warriors. But Craterus, who had now crossed the river with his fresh troops, closed in and mercilessly slaughtered the Indians. King Porus saw his men cut to pieces, but gave no thought to surrendering. In the elaborate, gold-inlaid war howdah atop his brave elephant, he continued to fight until he was wounded and could no longer wield a sword. He then joined the rearguard and shouted encouragement to his beaten, retreating forces. Alexander, admiring Porus' indomitable courage, dispatched Taxiles to persuade Porus to surrender. But unknown to Alexander Porus despised Taxiles, and even in his wounded state tried to kill him. Enraged, Taxiles returned to Alexander and begged him to kill Porus. Alexander was reluctant to agree, but realized he had no other choice. But before he could give the order, an old friend of Porus', Meroes, confronted the wounded rajah and convinced him to surrender.

Porus was brought before Alexander. The young Macedonian, well-muscled but of only medium height, looked up at the towering regal monarch and respectfully asked him how he'd like to be treated.

"Like a king," replied Porus. And Alexander, impressed by Porus' defiant spirit and bravery, promised to treat him as one.

Then Alexander, astride his favorite stallion, the 30-year-old Bucephalas (who died a few hours later from exhaustion), rode up and down the lines of his assembled army, praising everyone for their bravery. He especially praised his Thracian horse-archers, whose daring attack on the elephants was responsible for turning the tide of the battle.

King Porus agreed with him. And later, when Alexander had restored his kingdom and put him in command of all the territories east of the River Hydaspes, Porus persuaded a few of the finest Thracian archers to remain with him to teach his own troops their skills with the bow...thus introducing archery to India in the year 326 B.C.

The great Han dynasty began about 202 B.C. and ruled until A.D. 220. Under the Hans the Hun Tatar hordes were driven back to Turkestan, and Mongolia was added to the empire. Overland trade was inaugurated to Syria and Rome. Important political and cultural advances were made, including the standardization of the forms of Chinese written characters, the first definitive dictionary and encyclopedic history of China.

It was also during the Han dynasty that Chinese archers adopted the thumb-guard or thumb-ring as a means of releasing their arrows.

THE CHINESE

IN 140 B.C. the reigning Emperor of the Han Dynasty learned that the Hsiung-nu, one of several warlike tribes from Mongolia, was massing on the northern banks of the Yellow River with intentions of attacking a damaged section in the Great Wall.

The Hsiung-nu had been attacking China for over one hundred years. In fact, the reason that the Emperor Shih Huang Tu built the Great Wall in 214 B.C. was to defend his borders against the barbaric "devils" from the north. Ancestors of the Huns, the Hsiung-nu came riding out of Mongolia to make frequent, savage raids on Chinese stockyards and granaries. Like human locusts, they destroyed everything in their path. Astride their swift war horses, these nomads of the Gobi Desert and beyond made blitzkrieg attacks, showering their enemies with hundreds of thousands of arrows and then butchering all survivors with axe and sword.

Since the building of the Great Wall, most of the raids by the Hsiung-nu and other barbarians had been repelled. But now, with a section of the Wall badly damaged by an earthquake, the Emperor knew the Imperial Army would be overrun by the savage invaders unless the Wall was repaired before the attack started.

An army of workers was already frantically rebuilding the damaged section of the Great Wall, but it would be several weeks before the work was completed. Meanwhile, the Hsuing-nu had to be stopped before they crossed the Yellow River.

Summoning his finest generals, the Emperor ordered them to marshal the troops on this side of the river and to stop the enemy from crossing. All but one of the generals grew alarmed. No one could stop the Hsuing-nu from advancing, they clamored. Not unless one fought them from the ramparts of the Great Wall. To go outside the Wall and fight these devils, who aren't even considered human, was not only futile—it was suicidal! And throwing themselves on the ground, the generals begged the Emperor to be merciful and to spare their lives. Let the Hsuing- nu attack, one general cried. It is far west of here, and perhaps after they have massacred a few thousand peasants and robbed us of all our grain, they will return to their own country. The other generals quickly agreed with him. The Hsuing-nu weren't interested in attacking the Imperial Palace, they chorused. They just wanted food to feed their hungry, nomadic armies.

One general, Han Yu, who was younger than the others, stood in silence as he listened to the four generals pleading. Their cowardice and disregard for the peasants repulsed Han Yu, who was from peasant stock himself. But they were his superiors, and it wasn't his place to discredit them or disagree with their ideas. Finally, the Emperor ordered the groveling generals to withdraw while he made his decision. They quickly bowed their way out. General Han Yu started to leave with them. But the Emperor ordered the unusually tall, muscular young man to remain in his presence.

"How is it," the Emperor asked him when they were alone, "that you did not grovel or weep like an old woman, as your fellow generals did?"

"Mighty and most generous Emperor," Han Yu replied, "it is

simply because I do not agree with them." He went on to explain that he may not be able to defeat the Hsiung-nu, but he could slow them down. . .perhaps stall them long enough for the workers to at least repair the Great Wall.

"If that could be achieved," the Emperor said, impressed by the young man's calm confidence, "it would be considered a mighty victory. For once the Great Wall is repaired, our Army can defeat the invaders, as they have done in the past."

"If your most exalted highness will give me his permission,"Han Yu said, "then I will take as many archers as I need and try to stop the Mongols from crossing the Yellow River."

"You have it," said the Emperor. "Along with my ever-lasting gratitude, should you succeed."

Much to the surprise and delight of the four cowardly generals, Han Yu gathered his regiments and hurriedly marched out from the Great Wall, northwest to the banks of the Yellow River. The generals believed that this would be the last time they'd ever see Han Yu, as they expected the Hsuing-nu to massacre him and his army of foot-archers at their first attack.

And well they might have. But Han Yu didn't wait for the Hsuing-nu to attack. Instead, he attacked them, showering the advance party that had already crossed the river in boats with thousands of arrows in the same fashion the Hsuing-nu normally attacked others. Caught off-guard, the Hsuing-nu fell back and retreated across the river in alarmed confusion.

General Han Yu's commanders eagerly wanted to pursue them, but Han Yu ordered them to remain in position. Men on foot, he reminded his impatient commanders, are at a disadvantage when they pursue mounted warriors. Also, the Imperial Army was much smaller than the Hsuing-nu forces, and Han Yu knew his only hope of resistance was to defend their position along the river. For this reason, he had not brought mounted troops with him, relying instead on archers who could fight arrow for arrow with the expert bowmen of the Hsuing-nu.

But he did send spies on rafts across the river to watch for the returning Hsuing-nu. He also sent runners back to military headquarters for more arrows. Unaccustomed to this kind of warfare, archers in the Imperial Army did not carry large supplies of arrows as did the Hsuing-nu. And knowing his only hope of repelling the raiders was to keep showering them with arrows, Han Yu urged his superiors to quickly send him a fresh supply.

News of Han Yu's victory over the Hsuing-nu had already reached the Imperial Palace, and the Emperor and his courtiers were calling him a hero.

Jealous, the other generals deliberately withheld the arrows, hoping Han Yu would be defeated. They knew the Great Wall was almost fully repaired, and they hastily gathered their armies along its ramparts in hopes of defeating the attacking barbarians, and thereby gaining the Emperor's ever-lasting gratitude.

Meanwhile, on the banks of the Yellow River, General Han Yu anxiously waited for the fresh supply of arrows. Days passed. And still the arrows didn't arrive. Time was running out.

Across the river the Hsuing-nu had regrouped and were massing for an attack. Han Yu guessed the attack would come just prior to dawn, before the customary early-morning fogs lifted from the river. That way, the Hsuing-nu warboats and rafts would be hidden from the Imperial Army's archers. To stop this tactic, Han Yu had his men cut down trees and bushes and float them in the river at night. Then, just prior to dawn, he set fire to the driftwood and propelled the flaming logs and branches into the on-coming enemy. As their launched rafts and war boats caught fire and the alarmed Hsuing-nu forces leaped into the water, Han Yu had his archers shoot into the air so that the arrows came down on the unprotected swimming Mongols. Thousands were killed, thousands more wounded. The panicked Hsuing-nu swam back to the opposite shore, defeated.

Han Yu knew the barbarians would soon regroup and attack again, but by then he hoped his fresh supply of arrows would arrive and he felt sure he could repell at least one more attack. By that time, the Great Wall should be repaired and his task of stalling the enemy would have been accomplished.

But as days passed and still the arrows did not arrive, Han Yu grew worried. So did his commanders and his archers. Boyed by their unexpected success against the usually invincible Hsuing-nu, they gradually became more and more alarmed as they watched the hordes of fierce Mongol horsemen massing along the opposite riverbank.

Finally, Han Yu knew he could wait no longer for replacement arrows. His scouts told him that the Hsuing-nu had enlisted more tribesmen and now numbered over one hundred thousand, with more warriors pouring in every day. "We must fall back under cover of darkness," his commanders urged. "Maybe we can reach the Great Wall before the 'devils' realize we have withdrawn."

"And if the Great Wall isn't fully repaired, what then?" Han Yu demanded. "Would you risk the lives of our Emperor and our people because you, yourselves, haven't the courage to stand and fight the enemy?"

His disgruntled commanders reminded Han Yu that if their beloved Emperor would send them replacement arrows, they would gladly try to repel the enemy. But without arrows, what chance did they have of even putting up any resistance? They would be slaughtered where they stood.

"Have you no faith in me, your general?" Han Yu admonished them. "Have I not defeated the barbarians at every turn up till now? No, say no more," he added as his commanders started to apologize. "Merely obey me, and I will guide you to victory." With that, he ordered them to send men to every neighboring farm and collect all the hay and straw they could and return with it to camp as quickly as possible. Astounded, but not wanting to question Han Yu's orders, his commanders obeyed.

That night, under cover of darkness, Han Yu had half his troops remove their uniforms and stuff them full of the collected straw and hay. The stuffed uniforms, from a distance resembling live soldiers, were then placed in boats and on rafts. And at dawn, just as the fogs were lifting, the boats and rafts were set afloat and pushed out into the river by swimmers hiding behind them, to make the Hsuing-nu believe they were being attacked. At the same time, Han Yu had his men bang their war drums and cymbals and shout war cries, adding to the effect.

Immediately, the Mongols lined along the far bank fired volleys of arrows at the attacking Imperial "army". Their aim was

The Mongols fired volleys of arrows at the "army".

true and within moments the straw and hay soldiers had arrows sticking out all over them. The boats and rafts were also covered with countless arrows. And to the delight of the Mongol warriors, who sat astride their horses screaming and taunting their despised enemy, the Chinese withdrew their boats and rafts just as the fog lifted.

Believing them to be defeated, the Hsuing-nu clambered into their warboats and paddled across the river.

The Imperial Archers, hidden in the bushes and reeds along the banks, waited until the Mongols were in the middle of the river, then showered them with the arrows they had pulled out of the boats, rafts and straw soldiers. At the same time, more driftwood that was also hidden in the reeds was set afire and then pushed out by Chinese swimmers into the on-coming Mongol warboats. Rained upon by volley after volley of arrows, set afire by the flaming driftwood, the panicked Mongols once more swam back to the opposite shore, defeated. General Han Yu ordered his army to triumphantly display their victory banners and to beat their war drums. Across the river the Hsuing-nu, unaware that the Imperial archers were almost out of arrows, collected their wounded and slowly rode away. General Han Yu marched his victorious army along the hot, dusty, highway leading to the Imperial palace. Runners had been sent ahead to alert the Emperor of the victory, and tens of thousands of peasants and noblemen alike lined the streets to welcome the returning conquering heroes.

The only people who weren't happy to hear about Han Yu's success were the four Generals who had ignored his demands for extra arrows. Two of them had already fled, knowing that when the Emperor discovered what they had done, he would have them beheaded. The remaining two generals, Wu Ch'eng-en and Tsung Huang, swore they never received word from Han Yu's runner that Han Yu needed more arrows, or else they would have instantly supplied them. It was their word against the word of a common soldier, a lowly runner, and the generals felt secure that the Emperor would never doubt them.

But when they were summoned to the Imperial Palace, had paid their respects to the Emperor and praised General Han Yu for his wonderful victory, they received a shock: two of the Imperial Guard entered carrying the heads of the other two generals on the points of their lances. Wu Ch'eng-en and Tsung Huang gasped. But before they could speak, the Emperor held up a written confession signed by the dead generals, implicating Wu Ch'eng-en and Tsung Huang. They were led away, protesting, their fate sealed.

As for Han Yu, he was made general of the Imperial Army and became a national hero. He also became known as the man who first showed the Chinese archers how to use the Mongolian draw. For Han Yu had seen how accurate the Mongolian archers were, and how they wore a thumb-ring on the thumb of their release hand—whereas the Chinese archers released the bowstring with their bare fingers. The fingers got sore after a large number of arrows, no matter how calloused they were or how much they had been toughened by dipping them in brine. So, after the Hsuing-nu had ridden off, Han Yu sent men across the river to see if they could find any of the thumb-rings that had been discarded or dropped by the wounded. The men returned with several thumb-rings, some made of bronze, others of horn.

"You will learn to shoot with these," Han Yu instructed his best archers. "And when I am satisfied that you have perfected your skills, you will teach others who, in turn, will teach others. . .and so on, until every Chinese archer has become an expert in the Mongolian draw."

And so it was, as history has recorded, that during the Han Dynasty the Chinese archers learned to shoot with a thumb-ring, a style of shooting that has persisted ever since.

 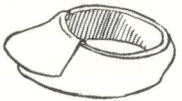

The Parthians were famous for their incredible horsemanship and prowess with a bow and arrow. They literally invented the "Parthian Shot"—an acrobatic method of shooting from horseback, while at full gallop, with the upper body twisted around so that the archer can shoot backward at pursuing enemies.

But the fame of the Parthian Shot pales when compared to what the Parthians might have been famous for—had their king not been a petty, jealous, envious man.

THE PARTHIANS

IN THE SPRING OF 53 B.C., the Roman consul, Marcus Licinius Crassus, invaded Mesopotamia with intentions of crushing the Parthian king, Orodes. Scouts had informed Crassus that the Parthian army was encamped by the Balikh River. Crassus was confident of victory, for his force of forty-two thousand men was comprised of seven veteran legions, four thousand foot archers, and five thousand Gallic cavalry that had been sent to him by Julius Caesar, who was campaigning in Gaul.

Crassus led his army across the Euphrates, and for three days they marched through the hot, arid terrain. On the morning of the fourth day, the Romans reached the banks of the Bilikh River near the city of Carrhae. Here, Crassus' scouts first sighted the Parthian army—an advanced force of nine thousand light cavalry that was positioned nearby on high, rocky ground. The cavalry consisted entirely of mounted archers, all using short, powerful composite bows and metal-tipped arrows. They wore no armor, only tunics, fur-fringed caps and loose-fitting trousers, and guided their quick, agile horses by a single rein and the pressure of their knees. They were superb horsemen, trained since childhood to shoot a bow while at a full gallop and from any angle, including backward.

The Romans immediately formed a compact hollow square, with the infantry in the middle and the highly regarded Gallic cavalry on both flanks. Crassus expected the Parthians to attack, knowing that at close quarters his formidable swordsmen would cut them to pieces. But instead of attacking, the Parthian cavalry rode to within arrow range and fired volley after volley of arrows at the close-knit legions.

Crassus, realizing his men were being slaughtered, ordered the Gallic cavalry to attack the Parthians. Both flanks charged.

The Parthians retreated, as planned, leading the heavier-armed Gallic horsemen away from the protection of the legions. Then, after a mile or so, the Parthians wheeled and split into two independent wings, circling on their swift nimble horses as they fired a deadly hail of arrows at the surprised Gauls. Half their number were killed before they could break out of the ring of fast-riding Parthian archers, and in hopeless disarray they fled back to the safety of the Roman legions.

The Parthians had not lost a man. Without rest, the mounted archers galloped to within bowshot again and began firing arrows at the hapless Romans. The legions stood their ground, suffering great losses as the Parthians rode around and around them, shooting salvo after salvo until finally they ran out of arrows. They then galloped back to the river, where a camel train, guarded by the rest of the Parthian army, replenished their arrows.

Crassus, realizing the battle would be lost if the Parthian archers resumed their withering assault, ordered his son, Publius, to attack immediately.

Publius eagerly obeyed. Commanding four thousand legionaries, and the remains of the Gallic cavalry, he charged down upon the Parthians gathered along the river. The Parthians rode out to meet them, but at the last moment wheeled their horses and retreated away from the camel train. The Romans followed, foolishly confident they finally had their enemies on the run.

As soon as the Parthians saw the camel train was safe, they again turned and split into two wings that encircled the Romans.

From the backs of their swift-moving horses, the Parthians shot volleys of arrows at the trapped legionaries.

Publius sent the Gallic cavalry out to attack the Parthian archers. But the slower-mounted Gauls could not get close to the Parthians, whose horses were chosen strictly for speed and agility, and were soon shot from their saddles.

Publius, cut off from his father's army, retreated with his infantry to a low, rock-strewn rise. Here, the Romans prepared to defend themselves against the circling, mounted archers.

As the unceasing volleys of arrows rained down on them, the legionaries tried to protect themselves behind their upraised shields. It was useless. The Parthians rode in close, their powerful horn-and-sinew bows driving their metal-tipped arrows through the Romans' shields; others shot at the legionaries' exposed legs, bringing down man after man. Finally, confronted by only wounded Romans, the archers gave way to the Parthian lancers who rode in and speared every legionary to death.

Publius and his officers fell on their own swords when they saw they were doomed. The Parthian *surenas*, or general, cut off Publius' head, mounted it on a lance and rode triumphantly back to camp.

Stunned by this devastating defeat, Crassus left eleven thousand of his dead and wounded on the battlefield and hastily retreated toward Carrhae. His advisors wanted to regroup behind the walls of the city, but the Roman consul insisted on putting more miles between his demoralized soldiers and the Parthians, and forced marched his army in the direction of the distant Armenian hills.

But dawn came before the weary Romans could reach the safety of the hills. And with the dawn came the attacking Parthians, mounted on their tireless horses, firing volleys of arrows at the hapless Roman column. The slaughter continued throughout the morning, with the Romans defenseless against their swift-moving foes who smartly refused to come closer than lethal arrow range.

By midday, less than ten thousand legionaries remained alive.

Crassus, the richest person in Rome and the man responsible for crushing the slave revolt led by Spartacus, realized it was over. Knowing he would receive no mercy at the hands of the Parthians, he plunged his sword into his abdomen and died in the arms of his officers.

Crassus' suicide prompted an immediate mass surrender. The victorious Parthians were surprisingly merciful. They offered life and freedom to any soldier who swore allegiance to their king. Those Romans who agreed were herded to the oasis city of Merv, located in the province of Khorassan. Here, they settled, intermarrying with local Parthian women to become loyal citizens.

The Parthian general, a fearless, brilliant young tactician whose name has been forgotten by history, was the first man to lead an all-cavalry army. His strategy of using mounted archers against infantry was also an innovative maneuver, and he returned to the palace of King Orodes expecting lavish praise for his swift, overwhelming victory.

Instead, the jealous monarch grew envious of all the praise heaped upon his young general, and within a few months of his return, King Orodes secretly had him assassinated.

Had this daring young general lived, he might have gathered all the Parthians into one mighty cavalry unit and destroyed Rome's power in western Asia and the Mediterranean forever. As it was, without his leadership Parthia never again achieved overwhelming superiority over Rome's legions, and was forced to wage an almost continuous war against Rome that lasted for two hundred and seventy years.

Neither the Romans nor the ancient Britons were known to be great archers. Their armies relied upon the sword, spear, axe, and other weapons to win their battles.

But after several notable defeats at the hands of archer-enhanced armies, the Romans were smart enough to appreciate the importance of the bow and arrow as a formidable weapon, and enlisted mercenary archers from other nations to strengthen their already famous legions.

THE ANCIENT BRITONS

IN A.D. 61 the main road north from Londinium was called Watling Street. Built by the Ninth Legion, who were engineers as well as soldiers, it ran to Lindum (Lincoln) and beyond, past Hadrian's Wall into Caledonia (Scotland). Like all Roman roads it was built to last, enabling their legions to travel quickly to the northern regions should they need to crush uprisings among the warlike Celtic tribes.

One such tribe was the Iceni, who lived in East Anglia and was ruled by the warrior queen, Boadicea. Until a year ago, the tribe had been ruled by her husband, King Prasutagus. But when he died from illness, and there were no male heirs, Boadicea by tribal custom became the new ruler.

Boadicea was a tall, large, full-breasted woman with long flaxen hair, blue eyes and a hearty laugh. She could out-drink and out-wrestle most men, and those she couldn't she took to bed with her. She was coarse, vulgar, and full of heathen cruelty;

yet, strangely, she carried herself with great regal bearing that made her a charismatic leader.

Queen Boadicea expected the Romans to respect her as the new ruler of the Iceni. She told this to the Roman tax-collector when he arrived with his soldiers at her village, Venta Icenorum. He only laughed and spat in her face. He then had her and her two daughters, Gwynnett and Ciara, tied spread-eagled to wagon-wheels and watched while his men whipped them and raped them bloody.

When the Romans left, Queen Boadicea swore revenge. Using her charisma, and a promise that she would drive every Roman out of Britain, she gathered all the neighboring tribes into one huge army and marched north and south destroying the Roman-held towns of Camulodunum (Colchester), Veralamium (St. Albans), and Londinium (London). 70,000 Romans and pro-Roman Britons were massacred by her army in only a few months.

During this rampage, the Roman Governor, Suetonius Paulinus, was on the island of Mona (Anglesey) with the Twentieth and Fourteenth Legions crushing a Druid uprising. That left only two legions, the Second and the Ninth, to engage Boadicea. The Legionary Legate in command, Quintus Petilius Cerealis, knew 12,000 soldiers weren't enough to defeat the Queen's 200,000 warriors and quickly dispatched word to Suetonius, begging the Governor to return immediately.

Suetonius forced-marched his legions east across the green hills and valleys that one day would be called Wales, joined up with the Second Legion at Glevum (Gloucester), and the Ninth a few miles farther east. The Ninth had marched with little rest from Lindum, where they were stationed, and were near exhaustion. But Suetonius continued marching throughout the night until his scouts returned and said Queen Boadicea and her army were camped only a few miles ahead. Then, and only then, did the Roman Governor halt his weary legions and order them to rest at the edge of a broad plain that was flanked on both sides by dense woods. Facing them, at the end of the grassy plain, were low green hills. And just beyond those hills, according to the scouts, was Boadicea's huge sprawling camp.

Some of the soldiers wondered among themselves why Suetonius had not ordered them to camp among the trees, where they would be hidden from the eyes of Queen Boadicea's scouts. But none of them were bold enough to question the middle-aged governor, for he was a cruel, ill-tempered man at best. As for the rest of the men, they were too tired to care *where* they were camped, just so they could rest.

Suetonius, meanwhile, although exhausted himself, gathered his commanders together and explained his battle plan. No one was to enter the woods until just before dawn. That way, should Boadicea send spies that night to locate her enemy's position, they would return to her saying that the entire Roman army was encamped in full view on the plain. Then, shortly before sunrise, the two cohorts of mercenaries—hand-picked archers of Scythian descent called the Cohortes Sagittariorum—were to sneak into the woods and arrange themselves in equal numbers on both sides of the plain. The archers were to remain hidden among the trees until the bugler trumpeted three times, signaling them to shoot. Then they were to shoot only at the charioteers—and to keep shooting until ordered to stop. "And any man who disobeys my orders," concluded Suetonius, "and shoots so much as one arrow before the signal, shall be flogged to death! Is that clear?"

It was very clear. And the Legionary Legates, Tribunes and Centurions bowed their way out of the Governor's tent and hurried back to their legions to instruct the men.

Dawn broke. The Roman legionaries, who had already breakfasted and taken up their positions on the plain, heard a distant rumble approaching. It was the sound of chariots and wagons being pulled by horses and oxen...of men marching and singing heathen battle songs...of war drums beating, horns blowing and cymbals clashing. And long before the Romans saw Boadicea's army, they saw the vast cloud of accompanying dust yellowing the gray dawn sky above the green hills facing the plain.

"Stand firm!" Suetonius shouted as his soldiers shifted uneasily in their ranks. "Remember, Rome is every man's mother

...wife...and family. His one true love. Cherish her...fight well for her...and she will always be yours!"

Even as the Governor finished speaking, two long lines of chariots, horses prancing, wheel-scythes gleaming in the morning sunlight, came thundering onto the plain. Each chariot was driven by a bare-chested charioteer wearing leather leggings. A fierce-eyed, tartan-clad, sword-wielding Celt chieftan stood beside him; while behind them, on the tailboard, was an archer with a straight-limbed bow and a back-quiver full of arrows. Many of the chariots carried an extra man—a spear-thrower who stood balanced on the chariot-tongue between the plunging horses. The war chariots reined up at the edge of the grassy plain, waiting for the mass of pagan warriors marching behind them to catch up. Behind the warriors came the heavy, creaking, ox-drawn wagons, each one gaily bedecked with fresh-picked flowers and filled with the families of the fighting men. While farther behind, on a green hilltop, stood the Druids—five old, bearded men in long flowing white robes, oak-leaf garlands crowning their heads, reciting ritual incantations to the Celtic gods of war and victory.

Suetonius, standing on a low hillock behind his iron-clad legions, viewed the enemy with weary, experienced eyes. Where is she? he wondered. Show yourself, Queen Boacidea. Let my men see you before the battle begins, so they may know they're fighting a mere mortal, not some enchanted heathen goddess whose magic can resist their swords.

As if answering the Roman Governor's thoughts, the two lines of chariots parted and through them came the Queen's gold-trimmed war chariot. It was pulled by two white, prancing, shaggy Celtic stallions. Boadicea rode in it beside her charioteer. She wore a gold breastplate over a deerskin jerkin, leather leggings, and a gold-and-bronze helmet from under which hung two long flaxen braids. Eagle feathers and sprigs from oak trees were woven into the braids, and garlands of wild flowers adorned her chariot rails. She carried her dead husband's sword, with its jewel-encrusted hilt, and as her chariot halted in front of the other chariots the Queen screamed insults at the Romans and wielded the sword overhead, the long gleaming blade flashing in the sunlight. Then, turning to the Celtic chieftans poised in the chariots behind her, Boadicea gave the command to charge!

Slowly at first, but gathering momentum, the double line of war chariots came thundering toward the Roman legionaries.

"Stand firm, men of Rome! Lock shields! Swords at ready!" Centurions and Decurions shouted their orders up and down the unwavering lines of legionaries.

Each soldier held his shield before him, its edges pressed firmly against the edges of the shields held by the men on either side of him, forming a solid wall of metal. In his free hand, each legionary held his short, bronze-hilted sword at his side, blade pointed outward, ready to thrust it into the first available Briton.

They hadn't long to wait. Led by Queen Boadicea, the Celtic chariots charged across the plain toward the legionaries. War cries mingled with the thundering chariot wheels and galloping horses' hooves. Once the chariots were within arrow shot, the archers on the tailboards fired volleys of arrows into the air. Before they could land on the Roman soldiers, orders were given and the legionaries not in the front line held their shields overhead, forming a metal "turtle shell" over their comrades. The pagan arrows bounced harmlessly off the shields. Then, by command, the Roman shields were again lowered and held forward and locked together to form wall after wall of iron.

But shields held by men—even Romans—couldn't stop the on-rushing chariots. As the foam-flecked horses and chariots plowed into the Roman ranks, scattering the locked shields, the first few rows caved-in. Men were trampled under. Swords and helmets went flying. Screams arose as the scythes on the chariot wheels cut off the legionaries' legs. But, somehow, the Romans behind them held firm. And despite the overwhelming number of Britons, the legionaries fought until they had closed ranks and driven the pagans back with heavy losses.

At the other end of the plain, Boadicea regrouped her war chariots and prepared to charge again. She was not surprised that the Romans had fought well; the Romans *always* fought well. But they had suffered their losses, too. And she knew that if she

Led by Queen Boadice the Celtic chariots charged.

kept charging and inflicting those kind of losses, eventually, by sheer numbers alone, she would be victorious.

Suetonius knew the same thing. But as he stood on the grassy knoll behind his legions and watched Boadicea's chariots begin another charge at his men, he controlled the urge to signal for his hidden archers to shoot, or his impatiently awaiting cavalry to join in, and instead kept silent. Waited.

The second chariot charge took an even greater toll on the legionaries than the first. The front four ranks were bowled over and ground under by the madly plunging horses and spinning chariot wheels. The fallen men were cut to pieces by the sharp, whirling scythes, and those behind them, as they again fought to close ranks, were killed by heathen spears and arrows.

But they did not die easily. Hacking and stabbing with their swords, the legionaries inflicted heavy losses on the undisciplined Britons and when Boadicea finally recalled her chariots, the blood-stained ground was covered with Roman and pagan corpses.

The Queen, believing that victory was hers, instructed her brewers to break open the casks so that her warriors could toast her defeat of Rome. Cups were raised, again and again. The mead flowed. In the hot sun, the wildly elated Britons soon felt the effect of the powerful, fermented honey drink and became drunk. Shouting war cries, singing battle songs, they clambered into their chariots and awaited their Queen's orders to charge.

This time, they would not be alone. Boadicea looked at the Druids gathered on the hill behind her. They stopped their incantations to "sign" that the gods were with her. Satisfied, she signaled to the thousands of warriors on foot to fall in behind the chariots. They obeyed with a roar that made the leaves tremble.

Suetonius watched the mass of blue-streaked heathens charging madly across the plain toward him, and smiled. This was the moment he'd been waiting for—and as Boadicea's army closed in on the depleted but unwavering ranks of legionaries, the Roman Governor signaled for the bugler to trumpet three times.

In the woods on both sides of the plains the hidden Cohortes Sagittariorum heard the trumpeting and aimed their arrows at the Celtic charioteers. Twelve hundred short, powerful, composite bows thrummed! Twelve hundred arrows flew at their mark. Then, with disciplined precision, twelve hundred more. And so on...

Charioteer after charioteer went down, arrows sticking in them, reins falling from their lifeless hands. Without guidance, the teams of galloping horses ran wildly out of control. Chariots collided, overturned, and were smashed to pieces. The Britons in them were thrown out, crushed, trampled or slashed by the scythes. Chaos ensued. The tens of thousands of warriors on foot charging along behind them found themselves blocked by their own chariots. They faltered, and immediately the thousands behind them charged right over them, trampling them underfoot. Then they, in turn, were trampled under by the thousands following.

From his vantage point, Suetonius now ordered his archers to shoot at the warriors on foot. At the same time, he ordered his cavalry to cut their way through to Queen Boadicea, who could be seen standing in her chariot amid the mass of confused warriors.

Finally, Suetonius ordered his legionaries to advance. The disciplined ranks marched forward, shields held before them, short swords stabbing to death everyone who stood in their way.

Boadicea saw the Romans advancing, and desperately tried to rally her men around her. But it was useless. They were being slaughtered by arrows from archers they couldn't see; trampled and crushed by their fellow warriors; and methodically hacked to bits by the steadily advancing legionaries.

The battle was already lost. Boadicea saw that even as she swung her dead husband's sword at the Roman horsemen trying to surround her. Ordering her charioteer to retreat, the Queen fought her way back to the rear of her forces. There, she made her two daughters climb into the chariot beside her, took the reins herself and drove uphill to the clearing where her Druids kneeled, heads bowed in useless prayer.

"All is lost," Boadicea told the High Priest. "Give me and my daughters the poison, so that we won't feel the shame of Roman flesh raping our bodies!"

The old Druid removed the Holy seal from a clay flask and

filled three cups with a pale brown fluid that was made from the common foxglove, the digitalis.

Boadicea embraced her daughters, kissed them goodbye and handed each girl a cup of poison. The third cup she kept for herself.

"Drink, my daughters," she urged. "Quickly, for the poison works slowly and we do not want to be alive when our enemy finds us." When Gwynnedd and Ciara hesitated to drink, Boadicea raised her cup to her lips and emptied it in one gulp. Then, handing the cup back to the High Priest, the Queen gently tilted her daughters' cups to their mouths and waited until they had swallowed the fluid.

"Now, sit beside me," she told them, pulling Gwynnedd and Ciara to the grass. "And we will die as you came into this world—together."

And as the Druids prayed over them, Queen Boadicea and her daughters sat cuddled on the ground, feeling their hearts beating irregularly. . .until all three eventually died of a fatal arrhythmia. With their Queen dead and their Druids in flight, the Britons lost heart; they stopped fighting and fled, themselves. The plain was covered with pagan corpses. Thousands more lay wounded and were put to death by Roman sword.

Suetonius ordered the corpses of Boadicea and her daughters hung from trees, so all of Britain could see their fate and never again rise against Rome. The Governor then gathered his legions before him and praised them for their indomitable courage in battle. Rome loved her legionaries as no mortal woman could. . .and those who had bravely given their lives for her, would be remembered forever.

Suetonius especially praised the Cohortes Sagittariorum for their skill and discipline. Their deadly accuracy had helped turn the tide of battle, and he promised to mention them favorably in his dispatches to Rome. Honored, the foreign mercenaries raised their bows overhead and loudly cheered the Roman Governor.

Roman arrows could not kill the Christian martyr, Saint Sebastian, whose body is buried under a basilica on the Apian Way at the feet of Saints Peter and Paul, and who is specially honored every January 20.

THE ROMANS

IT WAS AFTER midnight when Captain Sebastian entered the prison containing religious criminals and, plumed helmet under his arm, stopped before the heavy, iron-barred gate leading to the cells. On the other side of the gate the turnkey sat slumped over a table, head resting on his folded arms, snoring loudly.

"Wake up, damn you!" Captain Sebastian rattled the bars with the hilt of his sword, startling the turnkey awake. Bleary-eyed from too much wine, the old man picked up the oil lamp burning on the table and held it close to the gate so he could get a better look at his late-night visitor.

Through the bars he saw a tall, erect, muscular Roman officer in the Praetorian Guard, a handsome man in his early thirties who glared angrily at him.

"Open up!" the officer ordered. "I've come to interrogate the prisoners, Marcellus and Ennius."

"At this late hour?" the turnkey protested. But he knew better than to argue with the captain of the Emperor's own guard.

Grumbling under his breath, he reached for the keys and unlocked the gate.

Captain Sebastian pushed him aside and marched down the long, dimly lit stone-walled corridor that was lined on both sides with dingy, iron-barred cells. The turnkey followed him, lamp and keys in hand, still grumbling about being disturbed. Rats scattered before their approaching feet, the vermin squeaking in fear as they disappeared into holes in the ancient walls.

The prisoners locked in the cells slept on piles of filthy straw. The stench of unclean bodies and human defacation almost overpowered Captain Sebastian's senses. The foul odor was more pungent than even the most humble of stables, and the beaten and tortured prisoners were in worse condition than the most abused animals.

It made the captain ashamed to admit he was a human being. Here it was, two hundred and eighty-odd years after the death of Jesus Christ, and man still hadn't learned to treat his own kind with kindness or compassion. Worse; man was still being tortured, imprisoned and even killed for believing in anything other than pagan gods. Daily, the Emperor Diocletian issued countless death sentences to those "vilest and most insidiously dangerous rabble rousers," the Christians!

Captain Sebastian was a Christian, and had been for several years. But only his closest Christian friends knew it. That was why he was here, in the prison late at night, to visit two of those friends, Marcellus and Ennius, fellow officers in the Praetorian Guard who had been caught praying to their Christian God. Ordered by Diocletian to renounce their faith in Christ, they had refused. The enraged Emperor then imprisoned Marcellus and Ennius, and sentenced them to death by flogging.

Now, as Captain Sebastian stopped outside the cell containing his friends, he was revolted by the sight the turnkey's lamp illuminated inside the bars. Both young men were chained to the wall in a standing position, heads bowed, their naked bodies covered with raw, bloody welts and lash marks. Neither moved, and for a moment Sebastian thought his friends were already dead. But then Marcellus, nearest the bars, lifted his head slightly and worked his lips with great effort. "W-Water. . ." he begged hoarsely.

The turnkey laughed, muttered something about not wasting good water on Christian swine, and was suddenly knocked to his knees by Sebastian's forearm.

"Ignorant fool!" the Praetorian captain yelled at him. "How can I interrogate prisoners whose throats are too parched to speak? Now, go—get them water," he added, hand dropping to his sword. "Or your head will feel something sharper than my fist!"

Furious but too scared to argue, the turnkey hurried away. Sebastian moved close to the bars and called his friends by name. Both slowly raised their heads. Under their blood-matted hair hope glimmered in their eyes as they recognized Sebastian. He motioned for them to remain silent. Moments later, the turnkey returned with a bucket of water. Sebastian waited for him to open the cell door and carry the bucket inside. He then ordered the turnkey to return to his post and to wait there until summoned.

When the turnkey had left, Sebastian quickly held the bucket to the cracked, swollen lips of his friends. They drank greedily. But, when they could finally speak, they were more worried than pleased to see him. He should not have come, they insisted. If the Emperor ever discovered that Sebastian was there, he would know his favorite captain was also a Christian and immediately sentence him to death.

Sebastian hushed their concerns. As a fellow Christian, he assured them, their pain was his pain. He was here to share it with them; to comfort them; to reassure them that so long as they did not renounce their faith in Christianity, Jesus Christ would welcome them in heaven. . .

Marcellus and Ennuis looked at Sebastian, their pain-filled eyes bright with God as they assured him that they would never renounce their belief in Christ, no matter what the price. They then begged Sebastian to leave, at once, before his presence there betrayed his own religious beliefs.

It took great effort to speak, and their voices were barely audible, but the turnkey, hiding in the shadows beyond the cells, overheard enough to understand their conversation. Still angry at Captain Sebastian for striking him, the old man hurried away to report what he had heard to the officer in charge of the prison guards.

The officer, Marcus Honorius, was approaching retirement age and wasn't anxious to get caught in the middle of the furor he knew would arise once it was known that the Emperor Diocletian's favorite captain of the Praetorian Guard was secretly a Christian.

The Emperor hated Christians. Born Gaius Aurelius Valerius Diocletianus, of humble parents in the town of Dioclea in Dalmatia, Diocles—as he was more commonly called—had used the army to achieve greatness. When Emperor Numerianus was murdered in 284 A.D., the military chose Diocles, the commander of the Emperor's bodyguards, to succeed him on the throne. Diocles' first act was to kill Aper, the Praetorian prefect, to avenge the murder of Numerianus. Then, changing his name to Diocletianus, he marched against Carinus, brother of Numerianus, and decisively defeated him in battle. Carinus was later slain by his own officers, who were angered by his ineptness, and Diocletianus was proclaimed Emperor.

A wise and fair leader in most instances, Diocletianus soon stablized the state and the throne. Then, in 285, he appointed a Pannonian officer, Marcus Aurelius Valerius Maximianus, better known as Maximian, to the title of Caesar.

But Rome had lost much of its grandeur. Already Mediolanum (later called Milan) was taking its place as the capital city. Diocletianus, anxious to revive all the glory of the old Rome, insisted that everyone worship the ancient pagan gods. He personally adopted the appellation of Jovius, a form of the name Jupiter, and assigned to Maximian that of Heraclius, from Hercules. His regulations were oppressively rigid, and anyone found worshipping any other religion was ordered to renounce it or immediately put to death.

Knowing this, and knowing how fond Diocletianus was of Captain Sebastian, Marcus Honorius swore the turnkey to silence, then visited Sebastian the next day. He begged the young man to renounce his faith in Christ, or to at least deny it for the few remaining months that Marcus was still in service.

It was a generous offer, but Sebastian would do neither. The prison Prefect had no choice but to report the turnkey's charges to the Emperor.

Diocletianus refused to believe the turnkey, or Marcus Honorius, but had Sebastian brought before him anyway, so he could deny the charges. When Sebastian refused, and openly admitted to being a Christian, the Emperor was shocked and dismayed. He felt like a father toward Sebastian, and could not bear the thought of harming the handsome young man. He begged Sebastian to reconsider. Sebastian again refused. He in turn begged Diocletianus to allow Romans the freedom of religious choice. The Emperor refused; and grew angry when Sebastian tried to press the issue. He ordered Sebastian imprisoned for one week, adding that if the Praetorian captain hadn't changed his mind by then, he'd be put to death by arrows!

At the end of the week, Diocletian had Sebastian brought to his private chambers. There, Sebastian was bathed and given a pure silk robe and sandals made of the softest leather to wear. He and the Emperor then sat down to a sumptuous feast. They ate and drank wine and discussed affairs of the city. Neither man mentioned Sebastian's punishment or religious leanings. When the meal was finished, Diocletian said that he was considering leaving Rome and taking up residence in Nicomedia, in northwest Asia Minor. Naturally, the Praetorian Guard would accompany him and Sebastian would remain in command—on one condition: he renounce his faith in Christianity.

Without hesitation, Sebastian quietly refused.

The Emperor begged him to change his mind. He admired and loved Sebastian, but could not allow him to be a Christian. Sebastian tried to make Diocletian understand why being a Christian was more important than anything—even staying alive—but the Emperor only became enraged. Calling in the guard, he ordered them to take Sebastian into the public square and execute him.

"Use arrows, not the sword," Diocletian told the Captain of the Guard. "And make sure this Christian dog suffers!"

Sebastian was dragged outside, stripped, and tied to the flogging post in the middle of the courtyard. Then five archers stood in a half-circle a short distance away and shot arrows into Sebastian's naked body. The first four archers obeyed orders and shot at non-vital areas. One arrow lodged in Sebastian's thigh, another in his shoulder, the other two in his arms. But the last archer, feeling pity for his former captain, pretended to shoot his arrow by accident into Sebastian's chest, hoping to kill him.

Seemingly, it worked. Sebastian gasped out a final prayer to Jesus Christ and slumped in his ropes, apparently dead.

The Emperor, watching from a window in his chambers, covered his face with his hands and wept.

Sebastian's body was left tied to the flogging post overnight, so local citizens could see how Christians were treated.

After the initial curiosity had died down, no one paid much attention to the supposedly dead Roman. Everyone had their own problems. Daily survival in Rome was already hard enough for the masses without adding to one's troubles by showing undue interest in a dead Christian; especially since the Emperor might mistake that interest for pity, or mutual religious feelings, and imprison the sympathizer for being a Christian, themselves.

One woman, a devout Christian named Irene, did not share this fear, however. She was the mother of Marcellus, one of the two soldiers Sebastian visited in prison. Noticing that Sebastian was still breathing, Irene waited until after midnight, when the square was empty, then cut Sebastian down and carried his body away in a wagon.

Her small house was on the outskirts of Rome. Sebastian was unconscious but still alive when Irene drove up in the wagon. With the help of trusted friends, she placed him on a bed of fresh straw in her storeroom and nursed him day and night until he showed signs of recovering.

A doctor who was a Christian sympathizer paid daily visits, stitching the arrow-wounds and bathing them with medicinal disinfectants so they wouldn't fester. For several days Sebastian hovered between life and death. Then, his strength gradually returned and the doctor pronounced he was out of danger.

Irene's son Marcellus wasn't so fortunate. He and Ennius were publicly flogged to death and their corpses left on display so all Rome could see how Christians died. Irene and the family of Ennuis begged for their bodies, so they could be decently buried. But the Emperor refused them. And because of the way Sebastian's body had disappeared, guards were posted around the clock to stop anyone from doing the same thing with Marcellus or Ennuis.

The inhuman deaths of his two friends spurred Sebastian to a quick, almost miraculous recovery. Within a few weeks he was limping around and, despite Irene's protests, attending secret meetings at which he urged all Christians to unite and defy the Emperor. Afraid that he would be recaptured and put to death, Irene begged Sebastian to flee Rome. He refused, and instead doubled his underground efforts to convert more Romans to the Christian faith.

Months passed. Rome's decline continued. The Emperor increased his attack on the Christians and hundreds more of them were put to death in cruel, barbaric ways. Diocletian heard rumors that Sebastian was alive and behind the Christian resurgence, and sent soldiers to the city outskirts to investigate.

Sebastian, unafraid, wanted to confront them. But Irene and the other Christians, knowing Sebastian's power as a speaker and influence on the future of Christianity in Rome, forced him to hide in the city sewer until the soldiers left.

When Sebastian returned to Irene's house and saw how brutally the soldiers had treated her and her neighbors, beating and whipping them in their effort to find the truth about Sebastian, he became enraged. Taking Irene's wagon, he drove furiously through the city to the Emperor's palace. There, he presented himself to the captain of the Praetorian Guard and demanded an audience with Diocletian.

The Emperor was being bathed. Shocked that Sebastian was actually still alive, he wrapped himself in robes and ordered the guards to bring Sebastian to him at once. The guards obeyed. Sebastian's clothes were soiled and he still smelled of the sewer. But he stood tall and proud before Diocletian and angrily berated him for persecuting the Christians. He then warned the

Emperor that unless he changed his feelings toward Christianity and stopped worshipping pagan gods, he would have to answer to God for his sins in the after life. Diocletian, at first secretly pleased that his former favorite Praetorian captain was still alive, soon became angered by Sebastian's tirade and sentenced him to be beaten to death in public. The following Sunday, Sebastian was dragged into the arena of the crowded Coliseum and clubbed to death by three gladiators. Sebastian made no attempt to resist or defend himself, greatly displeasing the already unruly spectators. The Emperor, not wanting the Christians to make Sebastian a martyr—a catalyst that could swell the ranks of the growing Christian movement—ordered Sebastian's corpse to be secretly thrown into the city sewer.

But the secret was leaked to Irene by a Praetorian Guardsman who was a Christian sympathizer. Irene and her friends searched the sewers until they discovered Sebastian's corpse, and buried it in the catacombs under the Apian Way at the feet of Saints Peter and Paul. Seventy nine years later, in 367 A.D., Pope St. Damascus built a basilica over Sebastian's tomb on the Apian Way which became one of the seven principal churches of Rome.

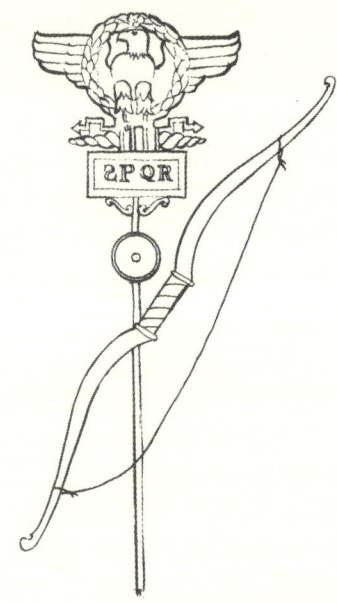

Aquileia was a Roman-governed city in the northeastern corner of the Adriatic Sea. In A.D. 452 it was the center of trade between the Western and Eastern Roman Empires, and later became known as a "Second Rome".

Although it had never been conquered, Attila the Hun was determined to destroy it in order to boost the morale of his warriors who had recently suffered a devastating defeat at the hands of the great Roman general, Aetius.

But, despite a long siege with overwhelming forces, the city withstood every Hun attack and may never have fallen but for a strange, freak occurence that Attila chose to use as a favorable "sign".

THE HUNS

AFTER THEIR bitter defeat by the Western Romans on the Catalaunian Plains in Gaul, Attila ordered his battered Hun forces to withdraw to eastern Pannonia. There, safe from their enemies, the Huns made camp in the dense woods lining the banks of the River Danuvius and tried to recuperate.

In the ensuing weeks, many of the wounded died. Those who didn't, found that their wounds healed faster than their pride.

Winter came and with it the howling winds and snow storms from the frozen north. The trees helped protect the Huns from the storms, and kept their fires fueled. But even fires couldn't keep away the intense cold. Huddled in the shelter of their tents and wagons, they wrapped themselves in sheepskins and the pelts of wild animals and ventured outside only to hunt, spear fish and tend to their livestock.

The weather worsened. Storm followed storm. Between the leafless, wintry trees the snow-drifts piled higher than the wagons. Often our herds and flocks were buried. Hundreds of animals froze to death. The warriors brought their precious horses into the tents with them. But despite their efforts and the horses' thick woolly coats, many of them also died.

During those devastating months, wild game grew scarce. A sudden unknown disease killed most of the remaining cattle, sheep, and goats and the Huns were forced to eat roots and rodents in order to survive.

Finally, winter melted into spring. The river thawed. The snows retreated and the winds became warmer and filled with the fragrance of rain-soaked trees. The warriors grew strong again and clamored to ride out and plunder their enemies' cities.

One day early in the summer of A.D. 452, Attila summoned his commanders to a war council. Scotta, Edeco, Orestes and the other officers gathered outside their leader's tent.

After a short while, Attila emerged to greet them. He accepted their respectful bows with a brusque wave of his hand and sat on a wooden chair that his servants had placed in the warm sunlight.

In his mid-forties, Attila was a short, squat man with powerful legs that, like all Hunnic horsemen, were bowed from a lifetime spent in the saddle. He had a large flat face, small, deepset eyes, a flat nose above a wide, thin-lipped mouth and a few straggly chin whiskers. His black hair was cut bluntly about the ears, and on this day he wore a sleeveless ox-hide jacket over a linen shirt taken from a plundered Roman caravan. His goatskin leggings were tucked into hide boots that had soft, pliable soles made to fit comfortably into his crude, roundish wood-and-iron stirrups. He held his powerful, composite, recurve bow in one hand, like a shepherd holds his crook, while his other hand rested on the wooden hilt of the dagger thrust through his belt. To his commanders, he looked rested and there was fire in his eyes and in his voice as he told them about his plans to invade Italy.

A week later, the huge force was on the move. Over three hundred thousand strong, the Hun army made the ground tremble and the skies dusty as they rode through the Pannonian provinces to the Julian Alps. The Huns expected the Romans to attack them as they crossed the Alps, for word of their approach must have spread ahead. But no attack came and, unhindered, the Huns rode out of the towering, snow-capped mountains onto the lush green plains of northern Italy.

To boost everyone's morale, Attila planned a series of easy, rapid victories. The first of these would be the capture and destruction of Aquileia, a Roman-governed city in the northeastern corner of the Adriatic Sea. Aquileia was the center of trade between the Western and Eastern Roman Empires, and later became known as a "Second Rome."

Attila's spies reported Aquileia was poorly garrisoned, and the Hun leader expected the city to surrender after the first charge. But despite being few in number, the well-disciplined Roman soldiers fought courageously against the overwhelming, screaming hordes and repelled all the Huns' attempts to destroy the gates or scale the city walls.

Determined to capture the city, which in all its years of existence had never been stormed or forced to surrender, Attila continued his siege of Aquileia for several weeks.

But no matter how many charges the Huns made, or how often their archers showered the walls with arrows, they still could not force the Romans to capitulate. The hordes of fierce-eyed warriors grew restless. Huns are nomads, born to wander, and patience was not one of their virtues. Especially when the countryside could not support a force as huge as theirs. Empty bellies increased the men's anger and frustration. Their discontent grew to near-rebellion. Spokesmen were chosen. They came to Edeco, Orestes, and Scotta, knowing they were the Lord Attila's favorite commanders, and demanded that they persuade their leader to give the order to move on and plunder less well-guarded cities.

The three commanders went to Attila and respectfully repeated the demands of the men. He listened quietly until they had finished. Then, eyes blazing, his harsh guttural voice thin with rage, he reminded them that common fighting men did not make demands of their king; they merely obeyed orders. And right now, the Lord Attila's orders were to besiege Aquileia. Then, washing down his anger with wine, he promised to make a decision about continuing the siege or withdrawing by morning. Edeco, Orestes and Scotta thanked him for his wisdom and understanding and bowed out of his tent.

Outside, there was a commotion. A scouting party galloped into camp with a small Roman caravan they had just captured. Attila heard all the excited shouting and joined Edeco, who was still standing outside his master's tent. The Roman military escort, six centurians, had already been killed. The civilian members of the caravan were dragged from their wagons, thrown to the ground, and made to kneel before Attila.

The caravan was comprised of an old Roman general, Flavius Augustulus, and his five servants. Flavius was balding and overweight, but he still carried himself with great dignity. Even when forced to kneel before the Lord Attila, the Roman held his head high and his expression was filled with arrogant contempt. He knew that he and his servants were doomed to die. But as Edeco looked into his proud brown eyes, he saw no fear. Just acceptance. It made Edeco admire him; and the wise, veteran commander hoped that he would be the one chosen to kill him, so it could be done quickly and expertly. . .and without malice.

There was one other person in the caravan who caught Edeco's eye: a young, muscular, handsome man of Parthian ancestry who seemed devoted to the old Roman. He, too, seemed proud and unafraid to die. And when Attila asked if anyone in the caravan spoke his tongue, the Parthian replied that he did, fluently. Attila ordered him to tell his master that everyone in the caravan would be spared if Augustulus instructed the leaders of Aquileia to surrender. The Parthian, whose name was Arsaces, obeyed. The old Roman immediately refused, adding that he and his servants would rather die than obey Attila's spurious demands.

Enraged, the Hun leader ordered Edeco to give Augustulus and his servants to the archers, so they could have sport with them before they were killed. Reluctantly, Edeco started to give the order—but was interrupted by Arsaces, who fearlessly faced Attila and demanded to be heard.

Scotta and Orestes leaped forward, swords drawn, intending to kill the bold young Parthian. But Attila waved them away and told Arsaces to speak. If the Huns weren't cowardly dogs, the

Parthian said scathingly, let the Lord Attila select a champion archer and pit him against Arsaces. Either in a competition of accuracy, or a fight to the death on horseback, using bow and arrow only. The winner to be granted any wish he wants, the loser to die. Surely the Huns, Arsaces concluded derisively, the greatest archers in the world, weren't afraid to accept such a challenge?

His words and mocking tone brought a roar of anger from all the warriors. Edeco realized this young Parthian was no fool. He knew no Hun wanted to be considered a coward, or afraid, least of all the Lord Attila. He looked first at his commanders, then at the angry horde gathered before him, then back at Arsaces. He then accepted the Parthian's challenge, told him to choose a horse from the herd; arrows and a bow from the master bowyer. "And then," the Lord Attila added angrily, " prepare to die...because no man alive can beat our champion, Breda!"

Breda was under Edeco's command. In his late twenties, he was tall for a Hun and had strong, sinewy arms that could hold a bow at full draw steadier than any other archer. Edeco knew Breda as well as any man (which meant he barely knew him at all), and he admired his courage and was greatly impressed by his skill with a bow and arrow. He was also impressed with Breda's knowledge of bow-making, an art that only a few men truly understood, master bowyers all of them, who had been taught by their fathers the secrets of how to correctly make composite bows; secrets handed down from generation to generation that explained the best method of gluing horn to the belly of the bow and sinew to the back; of reinforcing the tips with strips of bone and the handles with glue-soaked leather.

Breda had learned these secrets while living with his parents in a mountain village in Northern Pannonia. But he'd preferred fighting to making bows, and he joined Attila's forces while still in his teens. Before he was twenty he lost an ear in battle, and proudly kept his head shaved on that side, so everyone could see his "badge of courage."

Edeco went to Breda's tent and found him outside, nearby, astride his horse, plaiting strips of cloth into a lasso that he could use in battle. The two men spoke without dismounting, for Huns feel more at ease on horseback than anywhere else, and Edeco related the Lord Attila's decision.

Breda was pleased and honored that he'd been chosen as the Hun champion, and boldly assured Edeco that the Parthian was already as good as dead. Edeco was convinced he was right, and yet somewhere inside the veteran commander felt a twinge of concern, of doubt, and wished his warriors had never captured the caravan.

The combat took place on a grassy plain that stretched from the outskirts of the Hun camp to the gates of the besieged city. Tens of thousands of mounted warriors looked on, forming an unbroken line that surrounded the entire plain.

The Lord Attila watched from the wooden launching platform atop one of the siege-machines that had been stolen from a defeated Roman army. Several of his favorite commanders, Edeco included, stood alongside their leader...and when Breda galloped into the ring, followed by Arsaces, the cheer from the warriors rolled over the plain like summer thunder.

Breda and Arsaces, bow in hand, arrows rustling in their hip quivers, rode slowly toward each other from opposite ends of the plain. Hunnic horses are hardy, docile animals, with great hooked heads, protruding eyes, long bodies, and very long manes and tails. They have good stamina, are quick-footed and as agile as mountain goats. Edeco knew Breda to be a wonderful horseman, as all Huns were, so it was no surprise to see him gallop across the plain to within arrow shot of the Parthian, then wheel left, without losing speed, and shoot two arrows at Arsaces so quickly, the eye could barely follow his movements. But when Arsaces swung out of his small wooden saddle, and clung crouched on one stirrup on the opposite side of his mount while it galloped at full speed, Breda's arrows flying harmlessly over his head—every Hun, Edeco included, was shocked.

Arsaces then restraddled his horse and charged straight at Breda, shooting as he came. Breda never broke gallop, either. But he used his knees to make his horse weave this way and that, dodging the Parthian's arrows. All the warriors roared their approval. Attila and his commanders cheered along with them,

Scotta punching the sky with his fist in appreciation of such brilliant horsemanship.

As Breda and Arsaces drew closer to each other, one of Breda's arrows sank into Arsaces's right thigh. Again, the thousands of warriors cheered. Attila smiled and turning to his commanders, said it was only a matter of time now before the Parthian was killed. But even as he spoke, Arsaces pulled the bone-tipped arrow from his thigh and, nocking it on his bowstring shot it at the on-rushing Breda. It struck Breda in his left arm, causing him to drop his bow. A great moan came from every Hun. Dismayed, they all watched as Breda desperately wheeled his horse around and galloped away from the pursuing Parthian. Breda rode in a wide circle, trying as he did to pull the arrow from his left arm. When it wouldn't come out, he broke it off close to the flesh and threw the broken end away. As he rode back to the spot where he'd dropped his bow, Breda looped his left leg around the post of his saddle and leaned down so that his right hand almost touched the ground. At full gallop, he grabbed up his bow and swung back into the saddle.

The thunderous roar of approval that arose from the mass of onlooking warriors made the earth tremble underfoot. Within moments, Breda had wheeled around to meet his pursuer and was rapidly shooting arrows at Arsaces.

The Parthian looked surprised and dismayed by Breda's swift recovery. And as arrows passed dangerously close to him, Arsaces seemed to panic. Reining up, he whirled his horse around and rode off in the opposite direction. Breda charged after him, urged on by the roar of thousands of warriors. He gained rapidly on the dispirited Parthian, and everyone knew that Arsaces was about to die. Everyone, that is, except Augustulus. Edeco noticed that as the aged Roman watched Breda closing in on Arsaces, a slight smile of anticipated triumph appeared on his wrinkled face—as if he knew something the Huns didn't.

Edeco became instantly alarmed, without really knowing why; and even as he watched, Arsaces suddenly twisted his upper body around until he was looking back at Breda. Holding this near-acrobatic position while his horse galloped along, Arsaces quickly shot two arrows at Breda.

Arsaces quickly shot two arrows at Breda.

It was a classic example of what Edeco later learned was called the "Parthian shot." Both arrows struck Breda in the chest and buried up to their feathers. He made no sound but pitched from his saddle, dead before he hit the ground!

For several moments the only sound heard on that vast plain was the stunned, dismayed silence of more than three hundred thousand warriors.

Then Arsaces rode up to the front of the siege-machine and looked up at the Lord Attila. Blood from the arrow wound in his right thigh now ran down his horse's belly. But he showed no expression of pain as he bowed his head respectfully and asked the Hun leader if he would grant his victory wish. Attila was too angry to speak for a few seconds. Then finally, grudgingly, he asked the Parthian what it was that he wished for. The release of everyone in the caravan, Arsaces replied. And their safe conduct until they were beyond reach of any reprisals.

Attila drew his breath in sharply. His small eyes narrowed in his dark, swarthy face. For a moment, Edeco thought he would refuse. The veteran commander moved close to him and whispered that it would bring dishonor to his illustrious name if he broke his word in front of his warriors. He nodded, and spoke through his teeth to the Parthian staring up at him from below. One word was all Attila said: "Granted." Then, still enraged, he descended from the siege-machine platform and disappeared inside his tent. Arsaces rode through the ranks of glowering warriors and dismounted by his Roman master, Augustulus. The old General had tears in his eyes as he embraced Arsaces. Edeco did not hear what was said between them, but later, when the caravan had left the camp, one of the men told him that Augustulus had given the Parthian his freedom. Edeco was pleased. No man who could ride and fight as Arsaces could, deserved to be a slave.

It was not until late afternoon on the following day that anyone heard again from Attila. He then summoned Edeco to his tent. He was waiting outside the entrance, war bow in hand, and as Edeco approached he saw that Attila was deep in troubled thought. He told Edeco to walk with him. Silently Edeco fell in beside his unpredictable leader and without escort of any kind, the two men walked down the long gently sloping plain toward the besieged city of Aquileia.

There had been no fighting between the Huns and the Romans since the death of Breda. Attila had ordered all hostilities to cease. Now, as Edeco and Attila reached a small grassy rise about one hundred yards from the walled city, the Hun leader stopped and stared up at the cloudless blue sky. He remained this way for so long, Edeco finally asked him if something was wrong. He said no; that he was waiting for a sign that would tell him whether he should continue fighting or move on. Last night, he added, the gods who lived in his dreams had promised to give him a sign that would tell him what to do. Edeco was not surprised. The gods often spoke to the Lord Attila in his sleep and he always obeyed their wishes.

An hour passed. There was little wind and the hot sun made the two men sweat. But Attila never moved; never stopped staring at the sky. Most of the time Edeco too watched the sky. But now and then his gaze wandered to the city. He could see the sun glinting on the breast plates of the Roman soldiers on guard along the walls. They did not move either; but they were watching Attila, not the sky.

Suddenly, as the sun began to lower in the west, a great flock of white storks flew up from their nests in the rooftops of the city. There were so many birds, for a few moments they blocked out the sun. Attila and Edeco watched them in silence. The storks flew in circles above the city, some carrying their young, others just flapping their great wings in agitation; and then, as if at a signal, they all flew away from the city in an easterly direction. Edeco expected them to only fly so far and then return to their nests, because this was early in August and it was well known that storks did not migrate before the approach of winter. But the great white birds continued flying until Edeco lost sight of them on the horizon.

Attila smiled and a look of inner contentment came over him. The storks were the sign he'd been waiting for, he told Edeco. They foresaw the future. They were forsaking their nests and leaving a city that was sure to perish.

When Edeco didn't look too impressed, Attila added that he must not think this was meaningless or an uncertain sign; fear, he explained, arising from the things the storks foresaw, had changed their custom. Why should the gods say more?

He then turned and silently walked ahead of Edeco back to camp. There, once the rest of his commanders were gathered before his tent, Attila related what had happened. The men were dubious at first, but as their ruler explained about the gods in his dreams, and their promise of a sign, the hearts of his commanders became inflamed with passion and, as one, they fell to their knees to praise the greatness of their almighty leader.

Word of the "sign" spread rapidly through the camp. By dawn, every warrior knew about it and, emotionally charged, they stormed the city again and again. . .until finally its garrison was forced to surrender.

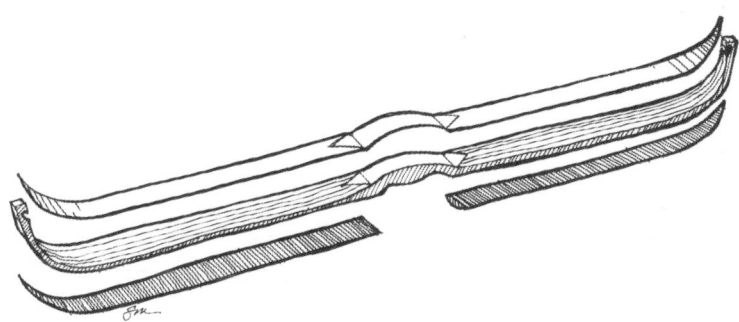

Bows and arrows were never the favorite weapons of the Vikings. They preferred a more savage and blood-letting form of fighting—hand-to-hand combat with swords and battle-axes.

Yet most Norsemen were skillful archers, whose forefathers originated the longbow and used it to decide the outcome of many historic battles.

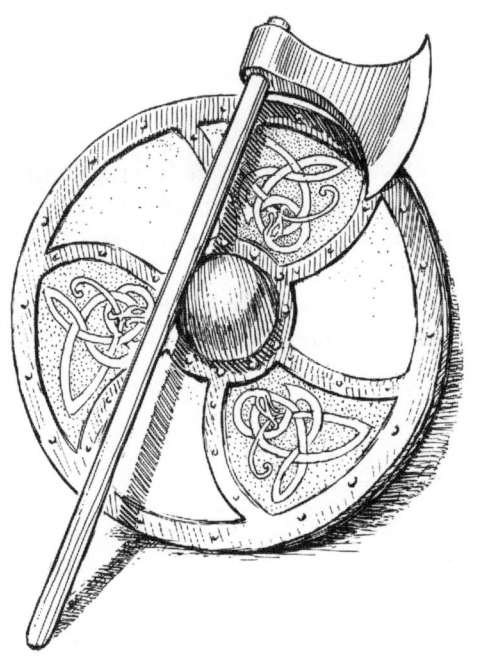

THE VIKINGS

KING OLAF TRYGGVASON of Norway, a ruggedly handsome Norseman of thirty with a full beard and long flaxen hair, stood at the stern of his royal dragon ship, the "Long Serpent," and watched the rocky coast of Vindlind fall behind him. Ahead, through a misting wind, lay a broad channel that separated Vindland from the remote island of Svold.

King Olaf hadn't sailed through this channel before, and had been warned by a local navigator that in certain places there were treacherous shoals and sharp rocks beneath the surface, capable of ripping the bottom out of even the greatest of dragon ships. With this in mind, King Olaf paid the navigator ten pieces of gold to guide them safely out to the deep waters of the Baltic Sea.

The navigator, a Vindland man named Sigvald, had also advised the King to send the smaller, shallow-draft ships of his escort through another fjord—one that was a short cut leading directly to the Baltic Sea.

"That way, sire," Sigvald added, "your majesty need not be worried that so many vessels in close quarters might cause an accidental ramming."

King Olaf saw the logic in the navigator's words, and with a certain grudging reluctance that came from being a Viking king in a turbulent war-filled world, split his fleet in half and ordered the smaller ships to head straight home. Then, bidding goodbye to the friends he'd been visiting, the Norwegian King and the rest of his fleet set sail behind the navigator's *knarr*, a small vessel that relied primarily on sails rather than oars and was designed for exploration and commerce.

King Olaf had enjoyed himself for the past few weeks, drinking, eating and reminiscing with friendly warrior chieftans, and today should have been in high spirits. Instead, he felt depressed; and even the reality of being aboard his favorite vessel—something that usually overjoyed him—failed to cheer him.

"What is it, my King?" asked the man beside him—a man whose huge size made even the robust king look small. "There is the look of black thunder on thy brow."

King Olaf stopped watching the almost seventy oarsmen seated rhythmically rowing ahead of him, and turned to the red-bearded giant, Norway's greatest archer, Einar Thambarskelfir.

"It's just a feeling I have, old friend. A sense of gloom...as if this is my final voyage aboard the Long Serpent."

"Impossible, sire," replied Einar. "Nothing can sink this mighty dragon ship. She is invincible."

King Olaf nodded, as if agreeing with Einar, and looked at the enormous longship with a mixture of pride and inexplicable sadness. For although he didn't share his thoughts with Einar, the King wasn't worried about the ship sinking; his gloom came from an uneasy sense of personal doom.

He had no idea why this feeling of approaching death was upon him. After all, his two enemies, King Skutkonung of Sweden and Denmark's King Svein, were not known to be in the Baltic Sea—and even if they had been, he still had sufficient warriors and longships accompanying him to fight off their combined attack. If he hadn't believed that, he would never have agreed to send the other half of his fleet ahead. Not only that, but the size and strength of the Long Serpent, alone, gave him a great advantage in any sea battle, so why he was troubled he didn't know. He also didn't know that the navigator, Sigvald, had been bribed by King Olaf's enemies to lead his diminished fleet through this particular fjord, into a trap.

Trying to ignore his uneasiness, King Olaf looked about him and tried to find comfort in the splendor of his ship. Usually, just one look at the Long Serpent sent his spirits soaring. And why not? She was beautiful beyond any mariner's dreams!

It had always been King Olaf's desire to build the biggest and finest dragon ship afloat, and two winters ago, in the Trondheim Fjord, his dream had become a reality. Stretching one-hundred-and-fifty feet from her high-curved dragonhead prow to her similarly carved snakelike stern tail, the Long Serpent was breath-takingly huge, sleek and seaworthy. Her bow and stern were ornately carved by Norway's finest prow-wright, an irascible genius named Thorberg, then delicately gilded. The great square sail was woven of wool in a double layer to withstand the fiercest of North Atlantic storms, dyed blood-red, and, in flagship tradition, emblazoned with the royal crest. She carried a crew of three hundred hand-picked warriors, had sixty-eight oar ports and room for every man's shield to be hung along her oaken sides.

Looking at her now, as with each oar-thrust the great ship surged through the calm gray water, King Olaf gradually felt his gloom overcome by exhultation. And as they approached the first bend in the channel, and the Long Serpent and its escort ships rounded the headland, the Norwegian king smiled for the first that day.

"That is more like my king," said Einar, smiling himself. "As thou hath said many times, sire—life is too short to waste even a moment on sadness."

"Well spoken," King Olaf said. "Too bad that mighty bow of yours is not a harp or a lyre, else I would have you play me a rousing song of--" He broke off, alarmed, as he saw an armada of enemy longships lined across the channel ahead.

"We have been betrayed, sire!" cried Einar as he recognized

Einar aimed and shot an arrow at the navigator.

the Swedish and Danish flags among the enemy vessels. "That lying Vindland curr has led us into a trap!"

"Shoot!" King Olaf shouted angrily as ahead he saw Sigvald's ship trying to out-distance them. "Kill the traitorous swine before another second passes!"

Einar, long bow in hand, jumped up on the side of the vessel. There, balancing himself, he nocked, aimed and shot an arrow at the navigator, who stood at the rudder of his vessel that was now several boat-lengths in front of the Long Serpent. The thwang of the bowstring could still be heard as the arrow struck Sigvald in the back and buried clear up to its feathers. With a single cry, the Vindlander pitched onto his face, dead before he hit the deck.

A great triumphant cry arose from King Olaf's men. Then, as the enemy fleet closed in for the attack, the various chieftans in the escort vessels begged the king to flee while there was still time. Although badly outnumbered, they swore to fight the Swedish and Danish forces, blocking them from chasing after King Olaf.

The King praised their courage and devotion, but refused to run. "Let the great god Odin take my life, if that is his wish," he told them. "But under no circumstances will I ever flee before my enemies!"

King Olaf then ordered all the vessels to be lashed together, fore and aft, as was the Viking custom in battle, so that they formed a single, massive raftlike bastion on which to fight. But the Long Serpent was so much longer compared to the regular-sized longships that her prow stuck out some forty feet, exposing the warriors fighting there to attack from both sides. There was no time to build any sort of additional barricade, though—even if King Olaf had wanted to—because the enemy longships were already bearing down on them.

King Svein of Denmark attacked first. His longships rammed into the lashed-together vessels of King Olaf. With a shuddering crash, boards splintered and sides of ships were caved in. Warriors on both sides filled the air with arrows and spears. The Danes hurled their grappling hooks over the sides of the Norwegian vessels, trying to lock all the ships together. Then, using their shields to fend off the swords and battle-axes of the defenders, the Danes tried to board King Olaf's vessels. But the Norwegians were too strong for them, and drove them back with heavy losses.

King Skutkonung of Sweden attacked next. But although his warriors managed to board two of King Olaf's outer escort vessels, they could not get close to the Long Serpent. . .and finally, unable to withstand the hordes of screaming Norwegians, many of whom had gone berserk, the Swedish warriors died fighting where they stood. . .their blood reddening the decks of the two longships.

But their fierce stand had seriously depleted King Olaf's forces. And as the warrior-filled vessels under Earl Eirik closed in, the weary Norwegians knew they had seen their last sunset and would be in Valhalla that night.

Earl Eirik and his men attacked the outer vessels first. One by one they boarded them, hacking to pieces the defenders, then cutting the vessels loose from the others.

Finally, less than one hundred of King Olaf's men remained. Desperate, the king consolidated his force aboard the mighty Long Serpent. Here, King Olaf and his warriors made their last stand.

It was a long and glorious fight. For over an hour the arm-weary Norwegians kept the combined Swedish and Danish forces at bay.

Much of this was due to Einar Thambarskelfir and his small corps of hand-picked archers. Balanced on the gunwales near the stern, they shot shaft after shaft into the attackers, tumbling them backward into the icy waters of the channel.

But even they could not fight off the overwhelming number of invaders. The battle raged on until there were only a handful of warriors gathered around King Olaf on the stern deck. One of them was Einar, who stood tall enough to see over the heads of the other warriors.

Spotting Earl Eirik fighting near the tiller of the vessel that had rammed into them, Einar clambered over the side of the Long Serpent and balanced himself on two broken oars. Then he took aim at Earl Eirik and released the arrow. The feathered shaft flew true, and would have pinned him through the chest. But at the last instant Eirik moved, and the arrow hit the tiller beside him with such force that it split the wood!

Eirik whirled around, alarmed, and saw Einar about to shoot another arrow at him. "Hit me that archer!" he cried to several of his own bowmen. At once they swung their bows in Einar's direction and loosed their arrows at the giant Norwegian. All missed, but one arrow struck Einar's bow in the middle of the upper limb, cracking it while Einar was at full draw. The bow broke with a thunderous cra-ack!

"What broke then?" King Olaf demanded, looking around.

"Norway, King, from thy grasp," replied Einar.

"Nay, not yet," cried Olaf. "Here, take my bow." He gave Einar his bow. The giant easily pulled the string back, then threw the bow down in disgust.

"Too weak, too weak!" he shouted. "This bow is not fit for a mighty King!" With that, he drew his sword and wielding it in both hands, charged his attackers.

Einar killed several warriors, then sank to his knees with a spear in his chest. "Goodbye, my King," he gasped; and pitched forward onto his face, dead.

King Olaf saw his old friend die and knew the end was near.

"Take him alive!" Earl Eirik yelled to his warriors. "I want his head!"

Hearing this, King Olaf decided not to give Eirik the satisfaction of decapitating him and nailing his head to the prow of the Long Serpent, and dived overboard. Several Danes and Swedes dived into the water after the King. But Olaf beat them off with his sword and clinging to his heavy metal shield, sank to the bottom of the fjord. There, he drowned. His body was carried out to sea by the tide...never to be seen again.

Few kings were more aware of the true value of foot archers than King Richard the Lionheart. He used them successfully during the Third Crusade, and was always quick to point out that without bowmen he would never have been able to defeat Saladin and his seemingly invincible Saracen army.

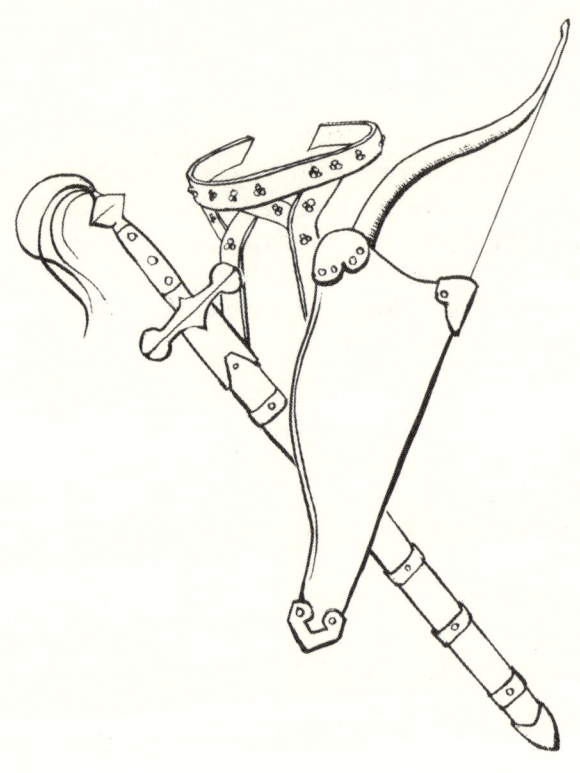

THE CRUSADERS

IT WAS AUGUST 1, 1192, the morning following the capture of Jaffa, Palestine, by King Richard I and a small force of Crusaders.

The English monarch, also known as Richard the Lionheart, was resting in his tent, talking with several captive emirs about the role that his archers had played in the victory. Although possessing only four hundred bowmen, Richard had placed them strategically on the flanks of his two thousand infantrymen, where they had shot flight after flight of arrows into the Saracens guarding the important seaport. Their deadly accuracy took its toll. The Moslems fell back in confusion, allowing Richard and his eighty heavily-armored knights to charge through their ranks, hacking them to pieces with swords and battle axes.

Richard, a tall, imposing man in his early thirties, with long red-gold hair framing his handsome features, paused in his recounting of the slaughter, then added that it was a year ago at the battle of Arsuf when he had first realized the true value of foot bowmen. Their consistently accurate shooting had caused havoc among the Saracen infantry, allowing Richard and his knights to win their first victory over the supposedly invincible Saladin, and the King vowed he would take advantage of their archery skills in every engagement from then on.

The King was interrupted at this moment by his young aide, Gwaine of Cornwall, who entered the tent to inform Richard that Saladin's chamberlain, Abu-Bakr, had arrived to discuss peace terms. Richard politely dismissed the emirs, wine and fruit were served, and Abu-Bakr was ushered in.

He and King Richard knew each other well from prior talks, and both agreed that the war in the Holy Land must stop. Abu-Bakr, speaking for the mighty Saladin, said that as Jaffa was now almost in ruins the Christian frontier should stop at the town of Caesarea. Richard, countering, offered to hold Jaffa and Ascalon as a vassal under Saladin. How would that system work, Abu-Bakr wanted to know, when the King returned to his native England? Richard admitted that he wasn't sure, which didn't satisfy the chamberlain, and the discussions continued. Finally, Abu-Bakr made Saladin's last offer: The Christians could keep Jaffa, but the coastal city of Ascalon, with its great fortress, must be held by the Moslems. Richard refused the terms. He wanted Ascalon at all costs. So did Saladin. Once again the talks broke down. Abu-Bakr returned to his master, Saladin.

The King conferred with his advisors. A large part of the Christian army had advanced beyond Caesarea, leaving Richard with only a small force to protect Jaffa. The King was sure Saladin knew how small his garrison was, and he ordered extra sentries posted to watch for the Sultan's expected attack.

They hadn't long to wait. At dawn on Wednesday, August 5, a sentry, who had fallen asleep at his post atop the city walls, awoke with a start as he heard the faint neighing of horses and the crunch of marching soldiers approaching. Squinting, he saw in the distance the rays of the rising sun reflecting off the weapons of the advancing Saracen army. In a panic, he descended from the wall, ran into camp and sounded the alarm.

The King and his knights hastily donned their armor,

grabbed their weapons and joined the infantry already mustered at the main gate.

On a level plain outside the city walls, Richard had his two thousand infantrymen set up a low palisade of tent-pegs to trip the Moslem horses. Next he ordered his men to join their shields to form a metal barricade, and to stick their spears in the ground before them at an angle to impale the charging cavalry. He then stationed an archer between each pair of infantrymen, with orders not to shoot until he gave the signal. Lastly, the King and his remaining fifty-four knights positioned themselves behind the infantry, so they could rush forward and help repel the enemy at any place that they threatened to break through the line.

The Saracen cavalry lined up in seven rows, each a thousand strong. During the Crusades, which began in 1095 when Pope Urban II urged Europe to recapture the Holy Land from the Moslems, the Turkish mounted bowmen had changed forever the world's idea of open-field warfare. Superb horsemen, their tactic was to gallop past the enemy lines, shooting arrow after arrow at relatively long range, until they had severely crippled their adversaries. They then exchanged bow for lance, sword or mace, and charged the weakened lines with such ferocity, they were seldom repelled.

Now, as the first line of Turkish horsemen charged across the plain toward the Frankish infantry, each man fired an arrow from his short, powerful composite bow. One thousand arrows flew into the air, momentarily darkening the sky.

Quickly, on King Richard's command, the infantrymen ducked behind their shields and most of the arrows bounced harmlessly off the wall of linked metal. A second and third shower of Turkish arrows was similarly deflected, with only minor casualties. But as the mounted attacks continued, gradually some of the foot soldiers were killed by the deadly, incessant rain of arrows. Others were saved by their coats of mail armor, but still suffered deep wounds.

Behind the infantry, the archers impatiently waited for King Richard's order to start shooting. But no order came and the bowmen had to stand there, bow in hand, arrows still in their quiver, fretfully watching their comrades-in-arms being shot down by the attacking cavalry.

From his vantage point atop a low hill behind the Saracen lines, Saladin also watched as wave after wave of his fierce mounted bowmen charged the Christian infantrymen.

But, despite their losses, the enemy never wavered. Saladin, a quiet-spoken, eminently chivalrous Moslem, admired their bravery and knew that they derived it from their leader, Richard Coeur-de-Lion. No braver soldier existed, and despite being opposed to what Richard stood for, Saladin respected the English king more than any other man, friend or foe.

But despite this respect, Saladin, whose full name and title was Al-Malik al-Nasir Salah ed-Din Yusuf (the king who brings victory to the faith), had sworn to drive the Crusaders from the Holy Land, or else to achieve a peaceful co-existence between Moslem and Christian. Because of this oath, and the constant hardships that the Sultan—a singularly simple, devout Moslem—had to endure while engaged in fighting the Crusades, Saladin was not a well man. Although only fifty-four, his shoulders were stooped and his walk no longer spry. He was still a very wise, articulate leader with a great sense of honor and integrity, who evoked fanatical loyalty from his followers; but below the simple white turban his dark, deepset eyes were no longer filled with fire, his long full beard had turned gray, and in his heart he longed for peace.

But, for now it was war—a war that Saladin was determined to win. At his signal, the Turkish horsemen exchanged their bows for swords, maces and axes and charged the Christian line. The infantry, similarly armed, waited confidently behind their joined shields. Behind the infantry, the long line of archers looked expectantly, pleadingly at their king for his order to commence shooting. But still Richard waited, motionless astride his big gray horse, eyes fixed on the on-rushing enemy.

The Turkish cavalry came charging up, their foam-flecked horses less than fifty yards away when King Richard signaled for his bowmen to shoot. As one, they nocked their arrows, pulled back their bows, aimed at the first row of charging Saracens, and released the feathered shafts.

Four hundred bowstrings thrummed. Four hundred arrows found their mark. Men and horses came stumbling, crashing to the dirt. Before their bodies had stopped moving, four hundred more shafts were winging their way toward the on-rushing horsemen. And a few moments later, as more men and horses were shot down, a third flight of four hundred arrows flew at the enemy.

Chaos!

Charging horses stumbled over men and horses already shot down in front of them. Men screamed as falling horses trampled over them. Other men scrambled to their feet, dazed by the fall, only to feel the pain of an arrow burying into their chest. And most of the Turkish horsemen who did manage to reach the line of infantry, tripped over the half-buried tent-pegs and plunged headlong onto the points of the spears sticking up behind them. Richard, seeing the Saracen cavalry in disarray, signaled to his archers to withdraw behind the infantrymen. As they obeyed, Richard drew his sword, spurred his horse forward and led his small force of knights into battle. The infantrymen pulled up their spears and unhesitatingly followed their King.

Richard's presence, fighting at the head of his men, threw fear into the hearts of the Moslems. Astride his charger, helmet plume tossing in the wind, sword flashing, white tunic emblazoned with a red Crusader's cross, he seemed to be everywhere at once. Inspired, the knights around him fought with equal ferocity. So did the foot bowmen, who had exchanged their bows for swords and maces. Together with the infantry, they charged relentlessly into the Saracens, routing them, forcing them to retreat along their entire front.

Watching from his vantage point behind the Saracen lines, Saladin grudgingly marveled at King Richard's courage. A man who never broke his word, the Sultan admired bravery and chivalry above all else. Even his Christian enemies, many of whom had at some time or other been Saladin's prisoner, were quick to acknowledge his fair and generous treatment of them. They also praised his simple beliefs and philosophies, refusing to accept that so honorable a man had been born a Kurd—instead insisting that the Sultan's real ancestors were a mixture of French nobility and English aristocracy.

The unfounded rumors did not please Saladin. He was proud of his Kurdish heritage, and anxious to prove that a man's integrity governed his convictions, not his ancestry.

Now, as he sat astride his fine Arab stallion and watched the Crusaders defeating his army, Saladin suddenly saw Richard's horse killed by a Saracen spear thrust. The animal went down, kicking and screaming, bringing the heavily-armored King crashing to his knees. His knights rallied around him. As Richard was helped up, and, sword in hand, began fighting on foot, Saladin's admiration was so aroused, he ordered one of his personal guard to gallop into the melee with a fresh horse for the King.

Richard acknowledged the chivalrous gesture with a wave of his sword to Saladin, then rode back into battle. His sudden reappearance broke the spirit of the already disorganized Saracens. Wheeling their horses around, they galloped back to the low hill and gathered about their spiritual leader.

Saladin, realizing the battle was lost, made his peace with Allah, and led his warriors into the desert toward Jerusalem.

The Crusaders watched them gallop off. Then, despite their wounds and weariness, to a man they thrust their weapons skyward and lustily cheered their King.

Richard accepted the cheers with a tired but grateful smile. "This day belongs to our archers," he said, indicating the small contingent of foot bowmen. "They're the ones who softened up the belly of the enemy, so we could finish the kill. Thank them!"

When the rousing cheers for the bowmen had faded, the weary King dismounted and motioned for everyone to get down on one knee. As one, knights, bowmen and infantrymen knelt and bowed their heads.

Standing before them, Richard held his broadsword aloft, the jewel-encrusted, cross-shaped hilt casting the shadow of a crucifix on the sunbaked sand before him, and humbly thanked God for the victory that every Christian hoped would eventually lead to the recapture of the Holy City of Jerusalem.

Very simply stated, Genghis Khan perfected the art of mobile warfare. With never more than two hundred thousand mounted archers, this Mongol military genius conquered most of the world that was known to him...and, but for his untimely death, would have surely conquered the few remaining countries.

THE MONGOLS

IT WAS A.D. 1227, the Year of the Mouse in the cycle of the Twelve Beasts, and a bitter, wintry wind howled across the Gobi Desert. The wind came in great gusts, blowing tiny particles of dry yellow clay into Fra Giacomo Ristori's lowered face. The Franciscan monk, a large, burly man of forty with a round jovial face, rubbed the tears from his stinging eyes. He then pulled the cowl of his robe across his nose, veil-like, and rode slowly on behind the small, shaggy ponies ridden by the surly Mongol guide and his youthful interpreter.

It had been spring when the jolly, determined monk left the Vatican, an emissary of peace for Pope Honorius III, who hoped he could persuade Genghis Khan to stop ravaging Europe. Fra Ristori sailed by boat to Constantinople and from there traveled over a thousand miles by caravan until he reached the southeastern tip of the Caspian Sea. Months before, a messenger had been sent to the Kha Khan at Karakorum, asking for safe passage to the Mongol capital. As a result, Fra Ristori was met by a Mongol guide and an interpreter, a lad from the Aral Sea region who'd been captured by the Mongols during one of their raids into eastern Europe. The three had traveled more than two thousand miles, sometimes with a caravan, sometimes without, and were now deep in the Gobi Desert.

Winter was approaching, and the cold was so unbearable that Fra Ristori had been forced to wrap his bare feet with felt and wear hide boots to avert frostbite. The robust, amiable monk was not used to riding, and every part of his body ached so badly, he had trouble sleeping at night. But he did not complain. His was a mission to save Europe from the "Golden Horde"—an army of fierce, disciplined, sheepskin-clad Mongol horsemen armed with bows and arrows who defeated whole nations, razing entire cities and slaughtering everyone who opposed them—and Fra Ristori was determined to accomplish his mission, or die trying.

Karakorum, the great Kha Khan's capital, or *ordu*, was on a high barren plateau without trees or hills to protect it against the incessant howling wind that whipped the sandy clay into a stinging fury. As Fra Ristori came within view of the *ordu*, he saw a vast plain covered with dwellings made of dried mud and thatch. Built haphazardly, with no thought of streets, they were surrounded by thousands of *yurts*—dome-shaped tents made of black felt stretched over a wooden framework with a hole at the top for the smoke to escape. Each *yurt* was mounted on a cart that when the Mongol nomads moved, was drawn by oxen. Lean hardy cattle, goats and sheep grazed on whatever grass was available, while enormous herds of horses occupied corrals with thatched stables. Next to the stables were graneries filled with rice and millet for human consumption, and tons of hay for the animals.

The squat, fierce-eyed Mongol guide, wrapped in furs upon his stocky, long-maned pony, led Fra Ristori between the *yurts* into the main section of town. They passed large caravanseries that sheltered travelers; ancient Buddhist temples; mosques; and small wooden churches built by Nestorian Christians. In Karakorum everyone was free to worship as they pleased, so long as they obeyed the laws of the *Yassa*, Genghis Khan's code of laws.

The guide reined up outside a small mud-and-thatch hut and indicated for Fra Ristori to dismount and enter. The hut had no windows, was barely high enough for the tall monk to stand erect, and even from the doorway he could tell how badly it smelled inside. He hesitated, not wanting to offend the guide, and asked the interpreter how long he would be housed here. The interpreter spoke briefly to the guide, then told Fra Ristori that it might be several days before the "Lord *bogdo*," would see him; meanwhile, this hut would afford him safety from any warriors who, in a drunken state, might forget the laws of the Mongol capital and kill him.

Trying to hide his alarm, Fra Ristori quietly suggested that the interpreter remain with him. The small, wiry, dark-haired youth seemed reluctant to agree. But after a brief conversation with the guide, he finally told the monk that he'd return after he had visited the *yurt* of a certain family whose daughter he wished to marry. He and the guide then rode off with the monk's horse.

Fra Ristori, carrying a bag containing his Bible and other possessions, entered the hut. Inside, the dirt floor was covered with ashes from a fire that had once burned in the middle of the room. Slabs of dried cattle dung were piled against the wall, and a bed of old, urine-smelling straw lay in a corner. Wind whistled in through the smoke-hole in the thatch roof. Fra Ristori looked up and, high above the hole, saw the cloudy, wind-whipped gray sky overhead. The monk shivered, chilled to the marrow, pulled his robe more tightly about him and prepared to start a fire.

The interpreter returned shortly carrying fresh straw for their beds, extra furs and a ram-skin coat for Fra Ristori. The monk, who sat cross-legged on the floor by a small fire, wrapped the heavy coat about him and continued warming his hands over the flames. Noticing how sad the youth looked as he spread the clean straw for their beds, Fra Ristori asked him what was wrong. The young man, Ogedei, replied that the girl he'd planned to marry had recently died from lung illness. Since she only had brothers, this meant that unless he quickly found another wife, he would sleep alone this winter—not a pleasant thought. He joined the monk at the fire as he finished speaking, and began drinking fermented mare's milk, called *fumiss*, from a golden bowl that bore the crest of the Chin dynasty.

When Fra Ristori saw the crest, he asked Ogedei how he had obtained the bowl. The youth yawned and said it belonged to his former master. Now dead, the Mongol bowyer had made bows for the Lord *bogdo* during the Mongol campaign against Cathay. And, as written in the Kha Khan's book of rules, the *Yassa*, all looted treasure was brought back to Karakorum and shared equally among every Mongol male—whether he fought or not. It was Genghis Khan's cunning way of making sure that his warriors didn't stop fighting during a battle to loot for personal gain, and he enforced the rule by executing any man who defied him...

The sleepy youth paused, yawned again, and his head slumped forward, chin on his chest. In moments, he was fast asleep. Fra Ristori took the bowel of *fumiss* from Ogedei's hand and set it down beside him. Then, weary himself, he kneeled and said his prayers. The monk then lay back on the straw, pulled the furs around him and tried to get some sleep.

Four days passed without word from Genghis Khan, and Fra Ristori grew restless. Then on the morning of the fifth day, Ogedei told the monk to accompany him to the Lord *bogdo*'s court.

Made of white felt and lined with silk, the huge domed pavilion sat apart from the other dwellings and was guarded by the Kha Khan's Imperial Bodyguard. The fierce-eyed, ramskin-clad warriors searched Fra Ristori and Ogedei for weapons, and finding them unarmed allowed them to enter the court.

Inside, the pavilion was draped with long lengths of golden cloth tied at the bottom with silken ropes. Hand-carved teakwood tables inlaid with jade and gold, plundered from distant palaces, encircled the fire blazing in front of the Kha Khan's throne. Nobles and ministers sat at the tables, drinking *kumiss* in respectful silence as their leader spoke with his chief minister, the Cathayan sage, Ye Liu Chutsai.

Fra Ristori and Ogedei threw themselves on their faces before Genghis Khan. At sixty-five, the man whose armies had conquered half of the known world was ailing and coughed constantly. He sat on the gilded throne of his deceased enemy, Muhammad Shah, the once-mighty emperor of Islam. Behind the Kha Khan was his royal standard bearing nine yak tails; at his feet, on his left, sat his first and favorite wife, a small pretty woman named Bourtai.

The Kha Khan was tall for a Mongol, powerfully built, with a flat nose and whitish tan skin. His blue-green eyes were deepset and piercing, but not slanted, and his long reddish-brown hair was streaked with gray. A full mustache drooped over his upper lip and his graying beard was shaved so that it only grew along the edge of his jaw and from the lower portion of his chin. The beard was carefully groomed and hung neatly upon the Khan's broad chest. He wore a long sable coat over his rough sheepskin jacket, coarse trousers and tanned leather boots. An albino hunting falcon sat perched on the Mongol's wrist; after stroking it for a few moments, he motioned for Fra Ristori and Ogedei to rise to their knees. He then had the slaves bring them silken cushions to kneel on, and bowls of rice wine, and bade a Ugur scribe with a roll of paper and a brush to record what was said.

Fra Ristori sipped the rice wine out of respect, then spoke through his interpreter, Ogedei. He praised the mighty Khan and gave thanks to God for bringing him safely through the wilds to the court of the Lord *bogdo*. He then added that the Pope and all the Christians of Europe had sent him to Karakorum to urge Genghis Khan to call back his armies and put an end to the war in the west. Surely the Lord *bogdo* had proved beyond any doubt that he could conquer any country he pleased, and already had more land than all the kings of Europe combined. Why did he need more?

The Kha Khan stroked his graying beard and said something to his wise old minister, Ye Liu Chutsai, who replied briefly. Whatever the Cathayan said, it made the Kha Khan smile with satisfaction. He then drained his cup of *fumiss* and told Fra Ristori that since God was the king of kings who ruled all of earth, it seemed only fitting that he, the Kha Khan, who was the Power of God on Earth, should rule over no less.

Fra Ristori started to speak, but the Mongol ruler silenced

him with a wave of his hand. It was his wish he added, that the monk accompany him on his upcoming campaign to conquer two hostile powers opposing him—the king of Hia, located near Tibet, and the ancient people of the Sung in southern Cathay. Before the dismayed monk could protest, the Kha Khan ordered the guards to escort him and Ogedei back to their dwelling.

A week later, Fra Ristori and Ogedei were riding with Genghis Khan as the aging, ailing Mongol ruler led one hundred thousand mounted archers out of the Gobi Desert to the northern slopes of Tibet. Here, along the *Nan-lu*, or southern caravan trail that was the Silk Route from Cathay to Europe, existed the robber kingdom of Hia. Comprised of predatory Tibetans and outlawed Cathayans, it was ruled by individual chieftains who paid homage to the warrior king, Temur.

Early in his reign, Genghis Khan had sent armies to subdue the marauding tribes. Mongol victories had been swift and devastating, prompting King Temur to send his youngest, most beautiful daughter to Genghis Khan as a peace offering. The Mongol ruler accepted the girl, and thereafter blood ties helped maintain an uneasy truce between the two kingdoms.

But six months ago Temur died, leaving his only son, Urag, to rule in his place. Showing neither fear nor respect for Genghis Khan, Ugar gathered all the tribes under the royal standard and raided the southern Gobi, putting to death every Mongol he found.

News of this premeditated attack by a supposed ally enraged the Kha Khan, and despite his age and ill health he did not hesitate to return to the saddle and lead his army into battle.

As he accompanied the Golden Horde, Fra Ristori marveled at the discipline and military organization of the Mongol horsemen. This was no wild mob, the monk realized, but a highly organized army divided into tactical units, or *tumans*, of 10,000 warriors. *Tumans* were split into *minghans*, or regiments, of 1,000 men; and each *minghan* contained ten squadrons, or *jaguns*, of 100 horsemen. All were totally self-sufficient, no matter how far they traveled. Each Mongol had at least two horses on which were carried a crude sleeping bag, rations of dried milk and powdered meat, and small tools that enabled him to repair his weapons in the field. Most warriors were armed with two powerful composite bows, capable of killing at 300 yards, and four hundred arrows packed into protected quivers; while a small number of "shock troops" carried a lance, mace, curved sword and a pike with a hook on the end to pull enemy horsemen from the saddle.

Protected by only a light armor of boiled hide that in winter was covered with furs and sheepskin jackets, the highly mobile, mostly illiterate Mongols were capable of enduring incredible hardships. On tough, sturdy ponies they could ride all day, for days on end, and then fight a battle without rest. When there was no food, they went without; when there was no water, they drank melted snow or opened a vein in a horse's neck and drank enough blood to sustain them. Harsh deprivation was a way of life that all Mongols were born into and accepted without complaint. Genghis Khan taught them discipline that, along with their mental toughness, made them invincible. The Kha Khan also perfected the art of mobile archery warfare, first used by their kinsmen, the Scythians, and later, the Parthians, developing his fierce, loyal Mongol horse-archers into the greatest offensive weapon that the world had ever seen—or would see, for centuries to come.

Fra Ristori, accompanied by Ogedei, was accorded the honor of riding a short distance behind the Kha Khan and within the protection of the Imperial Guard. From this privileged position, the jovial Franciscan monk could see everything that went on between the Mongol ruler and his military advisors.

Genghis Khan rode at the head of his horde, knees hunched up in the short stirrups, legs astride the high-arched wooden saddle of a swift black stallion. He wore an up-tilted white felt hat crowned with eagle feathers, and long pieces of red cloth that hung over his ears like down-turned buffalo horns. His full-length black sable coat was belted about him by a gold chain that he'd taken from the headless corpse of a Cathay nobleman. Watching him as they rode along, day after day, Fra Ristori found himself grudgingly admiring the mighty Kha Khan. For, even in his weakened condition, the Mongol ruler never showed pain or discomfort, and presented himself to his troops as an indomitable leader.

It was the dead of winter when the horde reached the snow-covered plains bordering the kingdom of Hia. Night was approaching. The Mongol army bivouacked beside a frozen river, and scouts were sent out to locate the whereabouts of the enemy. When they returned at dawn, it was to report that Ugar's force—more than double the strength of the Mongol army—was encamped in a valley two miles away. Hoping to surprise his foes, Genghis Khan led his army across the broad, ice-bound river.

Fra Ristori rode across the frozen river with the Imperial Guard. On either side of them, mounted horse-archers stretched out along the ice as far as the monk could see. The monk could hear the ice crunching under his horse's hooves, and when he looked he saw the breath of men and horses around him hanging, frozen, in the chilling gray dawnlight.

They crossed the river with only a few casualties—men and horses who had fallen through at places where the ice was unexpectedly thin. If the warriors were missed, no one showed any sign of grief. Horse and man vanished under the ice and those around him just rode on, grim-faced and purposeful. Fra Ristori, as any Westerner might be, was appalled by the realization that the Mongols held life so cheaply.

When they reached the mouth of the valley, King Urag's huge force—consisting of remnants of the Cathayan lancers, Turkic infantry, and all the armies of Hia—was lined up, awaiting the Mongols. The steep hills on both sides of the valley protected their flanks from any surprise attack, and the infantry was massed together in a wedge-shaped formation, with the mounted Cathayan lancers lined up on either side.

Genghis Khan, realizing the element of surprise was gone, had his warriors form six ranks in a single line, with wide gaps between the ranks so that the whole front was several miles wide. Then, the Kha Khan sent three *tumans* into the valley. Thirty thousand horse-archers rode until they were within bowshot, but still out of enemy arrow range, then they stopped and shot volleys of arrows at the massed ranks before them. The forces under King Urag wore only light armor and most of the infantry did not carry shields. The Mongols' arrows rained down on them, slaughtering thousands without a single loss to the horde.

King Urag quickly ordered his lancers to charge the Mongols, who retreated but continued to shoot, Parthian-style, as they rode away.

Believing they had the Mongols on the run, the lancers galloped after them. The Mongol horsemen led the lancers out of the valley, away from the view of the massed enemy infantry, and then suddenly wheeled to face them. Simultaneously, the rest of the horde, including the shock troops, attacked the lancers on both sides, cutting off their retreat.

The slaughter did not last long. In less than thirty minutes, every lancer lay dead. Without pausing to celebrate their victory, the Mongols reformed their ranks and rode back into the valley.

Fra Ristoria, forced to ride with the Imperial Guard, watched, horrified, as the Mongols again halted out of enemy bowshot and began firing flights of arrows from their powerful composite bows.

King Urag had no alternative but to march his massed infantry straight at the Mongols. Again the horse-archers withdrew, firing as they did, but this time only until the infantry was spread out in the middle of the valley, with their flanks no longer protected by the hills. Then the horse-archers fell back, and the Mongol shock troops charged the infantry, cutting them down with their short curved swords, lances and maces.

But by sheer weight of numbers the infantry held firm, and Genghis Khan saw that the outcome of the battle was still in doubt. Quickly, he ordered the *tulughama*, or standard Mongol sweep.

Fra Ristori, from his vantage point atop a low rise, watched as the outer ranks swept down on the infantry, shooting volleys of arrows from horseback, slaughtering the hapless infantry. Confused and demoralized, the remaining Hia soldiers fled in panicked disorder. The Mongols pursued them, mercilessly cutting them down until they had slain every man.

Realizing he was doomed, King Urag gathered the remnants

of his Imperial Guard around him and escaped into the mountains of Tibet. Genghis Khan did not follow the defeated Hia king. The Mongol ruler knew it would take months to track Urag down, and, since there were no more soldiers for the king to rally around him, he could killed at a more opportune time—say, when the Mongols returned to the Gobi Desert. Presently, though, the Kha Khan was anxious to lead his army into southern Cathay to defeat his old enemies. So, leaving a detachment of men to collect all the available, unbroken Mongol arrows, Genghis Khan led the rest of his horsemen southeast to conquer the Empire of the Sung.

But it was not to be. For shortly after the Mongols had crossed the Yellow River and made camp for the night, a messenger brought the Lord *Bogdo* word that his first-born, Juchi, had been killed in the steppes of Russia. Genghis Khan, seated outside his *yurt* with his commanders, showed no remorse at the tragic news.

Fra Ristori, standing nearby, saw the Mongol ruler's expression just tighten for a moment, and his blue-green eyes narrow as if in pain. Then he ordered meat and *fumiss* to be brought to the weary messenger, got to his feet and silently entered his *yurt*.

Later, Fra Ristori questioned his interpreter, Ogedei, about how long he thought it had taken the news of Juchi's death to travel the two thousand-odd miles from the steppes. Ogedei wasn't sure but guessed it had been no more than nine or ten days. When the monk scoffed aloud, and said he doubted if even a falcon could carry a message that swiftly, Ogedei explained about the the Lord *Bogdo's* cross-country messenger system, called the *yam*. It consisted of innumerable Horse Post Houses positioned every twenty-five miles, where herds of fast horses were kept in top condition. Riders wearing a belt covered with bells that could be heard ringing a long way off, galloped at top speed for as much as two hundred-and-fifty miles a day, carrying important messages from Mongol generals in distant places to the Lord *Bogdo*, keeping him informed of their every move.

"These couriers must die very young," Fra Ristori said, concerned. "All that hard riding surely has to destroy their insides."

Ogedei shook his head. "The messengers," he explained, "prevent internal injuries by binding themselves tightly about the groin, stomach, chest and head with thick cloth. They're treated well wherever they ride, and each of them carries a gerfalcon tablet that in sign describes who he is and what his mission entails, so that if his mount happens to break down, he has the authority to commandeer any available horse from any rider and continue on to his destination."

Impressed, and inwardly dismayed, Fra Ristori returned to his *yurt* to mull things over. Ever since he'd first met Genghis Khan, the monk had realized that the Mongol ruler possessed great intelligence, and was by no means the illiterate, godless barbarian that most Europeans viewed him as; worse, by so doing, they had greatly underestimated not only the Kha Khan's genius for military strategy but also his ability to organize and administrate—two key factors that had permitted Genghis Khan and his Mongol horde to terrorize and conquer half the known world. As for the other half, Fra Ristori had to concede that it was there, just for the Mongol ruler's taking, helpless to prevent itself from being overrun whenever the mighty Kha Khan so decided.

Wrapped in felt and sheepskin, Fra Ristori lay on his bed of furs and contemplated his fate, and the fate of all Europe if he could not dissuade the Lord *Bogdo* from his seemingly insatiable desire to conquer the earth. But, how to do it. . .that was the question. Silently, he prayed to God for assistance.

Two weeks later, the answer to the monk's dilemma became academic: for as the Mongols camped in a snowbound spruce forest, Genghis Khan weakly ordered one of his couriers to ride quickly to his son, Tuli, who was leading three *tumans* over the nearby mountains. The Kha Khan then retired to his white *yurt*, and gave orders for Fra Ristori and his interpreter to be brought to him.

The Franciscan monk found the Mongol ruler resting upon a bed of furs beside the fire, and instinctively knew the old man was dying. At once Fra Ristori began to pray for him, but the Kha Khan stopped him, and, through Ogedei, told him to listen carefully to what he had to say. A white falcon had come to him in a vision and said it was time for the Lord *Bogdo* to die—. The old Mongol paused, head lowered, eyes closed, and was silent for so long, Fra Ristori thought he was unconsciousness.

But suddenly, as if returning from a distant place, Genghis Khan opened his lidded, blue-green eyes and lifted his face to the monk, saying that it would not be up to him to conquer the rest of the earth. This task now belonged to his sons, grandsons and their children. He, the Kha Khan, the Power of God on earth, would soon be in heaven with the other gods. But before he died, he wished to give the monk a message to take back to his master, the Pope. "Tell him," Genghis Khan said weakly, "that it was ordained from my birth that the world should be ruled by Mongols, and there is nothing anyone can do or say to stop god's will. Now go," the old man ordered, waving the unhappy monk out. "Ride safely back to your master and give him my final message."

The following morning, Fra Ristori and Ogedei were escorted out of the forest by two Mongol guides. No one knew if Genghis Khan were alive or dead, for during the dawn hours his son, Tuli, had ridden into camp and ordered the Imperial Guard to surround his father's white *yurt*, preventing anyone from entering.

But as he rode, Fra Ristori was filled with despair. He had failed in his mission, and now must face the Pope with the grim truth: the Mongols were coming. . .and nothing, not even prayers, could stop them from ruling the earth.

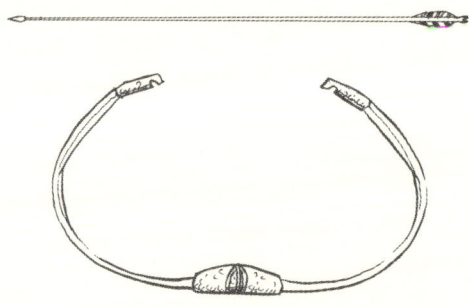

The English longbowmen, with stunning upset victories over the French at Crecy, Poitiers and Agincourt, firmly established themselves as the greatest archers of their day.

But bows and arrows did not win these historical victories. Archers did. Bowmen of humble birth who, as with infantrymen in every other war from time immemorial, seldom received due credit or glory...but were endowed with grim, unflagging determination, incredible courage, and uncompromising loyalty to king and country.

THE LONGBOWMEN

IT HAD RAINED hard all night and now, in the early hours before dawn on October 25, 1415, a cold drizzle continued to fall on the English army encamped in the French village of Maisoncelle.

It was not an impressively large army, considering that the goal of its leader, King Henry V, was to capture the throne of France. There were nine hundred knights, one thousand horse-archers and four thousand foot-archers.

On entering the village, the King and his noblemen commandeered the farm houses, cottages, barns and other buildings, while the archers took shelter under trees, bushes and any other cover they could find. Everyone was exhausted. Especially the foot-archers, who for seventeen days had marched steadily from the coast. Their clothes were ragged and dirty, and many were shoeless. Also, they had eaten little since capturing Harfluer, a well-fortified coastal town some two-hundred-and-sixty miles away, and their spirits were low.

It had taken King Henry and his army thirty-six days' of siege to force Sir Lionel Braquemont's troops to surrender Harfleur. Hundreds of Englishmen died in the fiercely fought battle. Many hundreds more contracted dysentery from the local drinking water. Over one thousand died, including the King's favorite bishop, Richard Courtnay. The sickest of the survivors were shipped back to England, while the rest marched through the hostile Normandy countryside under the most miserable of human conditions.

Will Bowman, huddled against a low stone wall with other archers in his squadron, pulled his cap of boiled leather over his forehead, wrapped his torn, mud-stained jerkin tightly about himself, and tried to forget how much he ached from that march. He was a tall youth, with unruly red hair, freckles, impudent blue eyes and a ready smile. Barely seventeen, he had broad bony shoulders and strong, muscular arms that could easily pull the ninety-pound longbow leaned against the wall beside him. The bow belonged to Will's late father, John of the Bow, who had proudly earned a living guarding the King's deer in the royal park at Richmond-on-Thames. The bow was Will's most treasured possession. Made from a single yew stave, it was almost six feet with horn tips and a strip of deerskin wrapped around its handle. It pulled smoothly, and could cast a 32-inch, iron-tipped, goose-feathered arrow almost three hundred yards. Presently, the bow was unstrung and its limbs were coated with a thin film of beeswax to protect the wood from the rain. But in a few hours from now, Will knew he would fasten a new string to the bow, march into battle and shoot arrow after arrow at the hated French army, now encamped a half-mile away in the villages of Azincourt and Ruissauville.

An hour before dawn the rain stopped. But there was still a bitter damp chill in the air. Will rose. Stretched stiffly. Stamped some of the numbness from his feet. About him, other archers did the same. A few examined their arrows, making sure the bodkin points were sharp and the heavy rain hadn't flattened the feathers; others strung their longbows with new strings or checked the old strings for broken strands.

Will squinted, straining to see in the misty darkness as he looked out across the narrow, gently sloping valley separating him from the French. In the distance, between the woods flanking both sides of the valley, he saw the enemy watch-fires. There were hundreds of them. Beyond the fires Will knew was camped a huge army led by the Constable of France, D'Albret. None of the English knew the exact number of the enemy, but yesterday as the weary foot-archers reached the crest of a nearby hill ahead of their companion knights, there, below them, the combined armies of France could been seen moving slowly up the valley toward Azincourt.

They were about a mile away, tens of thousands of mounted knights, armor shining, lances glinting, unfurled banners waving, followed by their retinues of esquires and pages, and then the infantry, wagons, cannons, and supply carts. They were so numerous, Will could scarcely believe his eyes. They literally filled the end of the valley. And later, when they finally formed into battalions, companies, and squadrons the front line of troops was only a half-mile from the English camp.

The French were so close in fact, Will could faintly hear their restless horses neighing and the voices of the noblemen, giving arrogantly confident commands in a language he didn't understand. Now, as Will looked out across the field at the distant French campfires flickering in the pre-dawn darkness, he wished he felt as confident as the enemy. But against such odds, how could he? Rumor had it the French outnumbered them by at least five-to-one, and it was considered a foregone conclusion that the English would be defeated. In his heart Will knew he would die before being taken prisoner. And as he heard the other archers praying and making peace with themselves, he realized that they too expected to die in battle tomorrow.

But there was a significant difference: most of the men had already proved their courage during the siege at Harfleur. Will hadn't. He had been too ill with dysentery. And now instead of having a battle under his belt, brave acts to recall, he had only the fear of the unknown; nagging self-doubts; would he be a coward or perform bravely when the battle began?

Will shivered, damp and cold to the marrow of his bones. He looked down the muddy lane that ran through the village and saw a sentry silhouetted against one of the watch-fires. Will envied the man. He wished he could warm himself by the fire. But the men had been given strict orders to remain still and quiet until dawn. Everyone obeyed. . .the only noise being an occasional sleepy grunt or the sound of someone snoring.

Pale gray streaks in the sky indicated that dawn was approaching. Will yawned. He was still tired, but a night's rest had returned most of his strength and revived his flagging spirits. Hunkering down by the wall, he leaned his head back, closed his eyes and tried to get some last-minute sleep.

It was impossible. His mind churned too fast. All he could think of was the upcoming battle, and how he mustn't disgrace himself and dishonor his father's good name.

Shortly after dawn, it started raining again. The already soft, muddy ground became even muddier; especially the half-mile stretch of tree-lined field separating the French and English forces. The field had been recently plowed and sewn with corn, and now, after the steady, heavy rain, it was a sea of knee-deep mud.

Young King Henry, only twenty eight, realized the mud was to his advantage; the thousands of French knights, encased in heavy armor, would have difficulty maneuvering their horses in the slippery mire. Also, according to the king's scouts, many of the French noblemen hadn't dismounted during the night, deciding it was better to remain on horseback than to lie down in armor in the mud. They, and their restless horses, were weary from the all-night vigil. And even the knights who had dismounted, hadn't removed their armor or the heavy protective trappings on their horses, and none were as fresh as the now-rested English troops.

Just knowing this, boosted the king's confidence about his chances of a victory. And when Sir Walter Hungerford told Henry that he wished they had ten thousand more of England's best archers with them, the fiery young king told him not to be foolish. His hope was in God, in whom he trusted for victory. And he would not, even if he could, increase his forces by a single man. For if it was the pleasure of the Almighty, few as his followers were, they were sufficient to chastise the confidence of the enemy, who relied on their numbers. Numbers which, he added, would prevent the French from moving freely in the space of the tree-lined battlefield afforded them. The truth was, he would feel less confident of victory if the French were half their number, because then they would have the advantage of maneuverability.

At daylight, King Henry and his army breakfasted on cooked meat and wine. The portions were paltry and there was no bread. Wild hazelnuts helped dull the English appetites, but after days of empty bellies most of the men were still hungry. Wanting his men to fight while their strength was up, the king quickly gave the order to muster.

With rain slanting down from the cloudy gray sky, the English formed into three large groups. A priest gave mass to each group, so that all might hear his blessings. Then the priests and the baggage were sent to the rear with the horses, guarded by ten knights and twenty archers.

On the battlefield the English men-at-arms formed into three battalions. King Henry commanded the main body, while the Duke of York and Lord Camoys commanded the left and right wings, respectively. The archers were placed between the wings, in the form of a wedge. The young king, mounted on a small gray horse and wearing a gold, bejeweled crown, gleaming armor and a surcoat embroidered with the leopards of England and the *fleurs-de-lis* of France, rode along the lines and addressed his men with great spirit. He had come to France, he told them, to recover his lawful inheritance. It was a fair and just claim, and as his subjects they should be proud to fight for their king. Remember, also, that they were born in England, where their wives, children and parents still lived, and therefore should strive to return with fame and glory. He added that the kings of England, his predecessors, had gained many noble victories over the French; and he reminded the men how their enemies had boasted they would cut off three fingers from the right hand of every archer they took prisoner, so that they would never again kill man or horse!

Will, listening to the king's stirring speech with the other archers, felt encouraged and cheered along with everyone else.

"Sire," he called out as King Henry rode past, "we pray God give you a good life, and the victory over your enemies!"

Other men took up the shout, repeating it again and again. The young king smiled and waved his gauntlet in response. Then he rode back to his noblemen, dismounted, and prepared for the enemy attack.

Instead, French negotiators approached. They proposed to the king that if he would renounce his false claim to the crown of France and restore the town of Harfluer, he could retain all the land he held by ancient conquest in Picardy. Finding their proposal unsuitable, Henry stated his own terms: If the King of France gave him the Duchy of Guienne, and the five towns which ought to form part of that province, together with the Comte of Ponthieu, and the Princess Katherine's hand in marriage along with eight hundred thousand crowns for her jewels and apparel, he would relinquish his title to the French crown and give up Harfleur.

Angered by his bold demands, the negotiators rejected Henry's offer and returned to their camp. Realizing that all hope of peace had vanished, the king renewed his preparations for battle.

But again no attack materialized. Both armies waited for the other to make the first move. The morning dragged by. King Henry's confidence began to waver. With each passing hour his men were growing hungrier and weaker. Guessing the French must know this, the king decided to attack and gave Sir Thomas Erpingham the honor of announcing it the archers. The venerable white-haired Knight of the Garter drew up before the men, who stood leaning on their longbows, and threw his baton into the air.

"Now strike!" he exclaimed.

The archers answered with a loud cheer. And as the King gave the order, "Banners advance!" the men immediately knelt and prayed for the Almighty to protect them. Then each man put a piece of dirt in his mouth to remind himself that he was mortal and of this earth, and marched toward the enemy lines.

Will was in the front rank. He trudged through the deep mud, longbow in one hand and a six-foot stake, pointed at both ends, in the other. Alongside him the other archers carried similar stakes. Ahead, Will could see the French knights massed and waiting at the end of the field. His heart pounded. His mouth felt dry. There was the coppery taste of fear when he tried to swallow. But he pressed on bravely, telling himself that there was no better or more honorable way to die than for one's king and country.

The Constable of France watched the English advancing. He felt secure knowing he had a great advantage in numbers, and secretly hoped the battle was a memorable one so his name would be enshrined forever in history.

In front of him the mounted French knights also watched the English archers marching toward them. They were massed together so tightly, they barely had room to raise their weapons.

Earlier, in order to gain distinction in the upcoming battle, the knights had argued pettily amongst themselves, each feeling he should have the honor of leading the first charge. Personal glory was uppermost in each nobleman's mind. Arrogantly confident of victory, they pushed themselves in front of the foot-soldiers and Flemish crossbowmen, rendering them useless. Then, as the "flower of French nobility" saw the poorly dressed English archers drawing closer, they eagerly couched their lances and prepared to charge.

But they were so numerous, and their lines were so cramped together, they had trouble moving forward. And when they finally did, they found their horses kept floundering in the deep mud.

At extreme bowshot the English archers halted and the men in the front line drove their stakes into the ground, with the points facing outward to protect them from the French cavalry. Then, upon command, Will and every other archer nocked an arrow, pulled back the string until his hand was beside his ear, aimed, and shot at the French knights massed before them.

The twang of four thousand bowstrings was followed by the hiss of the launched arrows. Momentarily, the sky was darkened by so many shafts.

Will watched the arrows land among the massed French knights. Most struck the knights on their helmets and vizors.

Will continued firing arrow after arrow.

Many fell shot through the brain. Others leaned forward, heads ducked to avoid the deadly rain of arrows. Shaken by the sight of so many men killed, Will just stood there and stared, open-mouthed, at the distant slaughter.

"Shoot, lad!" Roger Greenleaf urged Will. "Loose another shaft!"

Will snapped out of his reverie and obeyed. He and the other archers continued firing arrow after arrow at the tightly massed French knights.

The Flemish crossbowmen tried to discharge their bolts at the English, but they were so impeded by the milling horses of the wounded knights that after one volley, they had to retire to the rear or risk being trampled to death.

The Constable of France, realizing that his men were being slaughtered, gave the order to attack.

Sir Clignet de Brabant, Admiral of France, led the first charge with twelve hundred men-at-arms. But the English archers stood their ground and fired volleys of arrows at them. Some deliberately aimed at the horses, causing them to stumble and swerve from their course. Unable to control the pain-maddened horses, the knights collided with each other, adding to the confusion. And when the French charge finally reached the fence of stakes in front of the archers, only one hundred-and-fifty knights remained. And these were repelled by the stakes.

The archers continued to shoot with deadly accuracy. At this short range the bodkin-headed arrows pierced even the finest armor. Knight after knight fell, dead, forcing the French to retreat in panic. Some of the horses plunged into the sharp-pointed stakes, badly wounding them. The injured horses reared up, pitching their riders from the saddle.

King Henry, seeing the disorganized retreat, ordered his men to advance. The archers slung their bows behind their backs, drew their axes and billhooks and attacked the fallen French knights. All were killed, with very few English casualties.

Meanwhile, the retreating knights collided with the knights making the next charge. Chaos ensued. Horses lost their footing in the knee-deep mire. Knights were knocked to the ground. Hundreds were trampled to death. Others, unable to move in their heavy armor, lay face-down in the mud and suffocated. Panic and confusion slowed down the charge, making the trapped knights easy targets for the English archers.

"Hear me, my lords," King Henry told the dismounted knights about him. "Our brave archers have done their share. Now it's our turn!" Drawing his sword, he led his eager men toward the floundering enemy.

The French put up little resistance. Most were slaughtered. Those who weren't killed retreated in total disarray. Will and the other archers shot volley after volley of arrows at the fleeing men-at-arms. Hundreds died in their tracks. Hundreds more were wounded and left to die by their panicked companions. The muddy field grew red from spilled French blood. Finally, the archers exhausted their arrows. Slinging their bows behind them, they drew their weapons and prepared for hand-to-hand fighting.

Encouraged by their early victory, King Henry led his men into the main body of French knights still massed about the Constable. Although shocked by the sudden, overwhelming success of the English, the knights fought back. But again they were impeded by their tightly wedged ranks and had difficulty wielding their weapons. By sheer numbers alone, however, they withstood the English attack.

The battle raged fiercely for over an hour. No man asked for quarter; none gave any. Not even Will. Caught up in the excitment of the battle, he fought fearlessly alongside his fellow archers. There was no time to think; to worry; to be afraid. At such close quarters, it was either kill or be killed. And Will swung his axe with the skill and ferocity of an experienced veteran.

At the height of the battle, several French knights from the retinue of the Lord of Croye fought their way close to King Henry. One of them struck him on the head with a mace, beating him to his knees. For a critical moment, the dazed king seemed lost. Then his knights rallied. Closing in around their king, they fought off his assailants, killing most of them.

But the danger wasn't over. Before young Henry or his men could even lower their swords, the Duke of Alencon and his knights cut their way to the royal banner. The French Duke killed the Duke of York with his battle-axe, then attacked the king.

Henry fought back. The Duke of Alencon swung his battle-axe again, clipping off part of the crown the king wore around his helmet. The king staggered back. But before the Duke could strike again, one of the king's knights pushed between them and killed the French nobleman with his sword.

Dismayed by the Duke's death, his followers withdrew in disarray. Their retreat shattered the spirit of the remaining French knights and they fell back in panic. As King Henry led his men after them, he heard shouts of alarm coming from his rear. Two French knights and a small band of armed peasants had worked their way to the rear of the English army and were attacking the soldiers guarding the baggage. King Henry, not knowing the size of the French force, thought it was the expected reinforcements under the Duke of Brittany. So did the main body of French knights under the Constable and, cheered by the thought, they stopped retreating and turned to face King Henry's troops. Thinking that he was being attacked from both directions by a superior force, the young king ordered his men to kill all the prisoners and the wounded, so they could not fight against him. When his regular soldiers refused to obey the command, Henry had his own guard do the job. Reluctantly, they obeyed. And hundreds of helpless French knights were killed before the king realized his mistake and stopped the ignoble slaughter.

Meanwhile, at the far end of the battlefield, the Constable was killed. With their leader dead, all French resistance ended. And the remaining French force retreated in panicked disarray.

The battle was over. Victory belonged to King Henry.

Will, weary from fighting, sat among the other archers and gave thanks to the Almighty for sparing him. Before him in all directions the field was covered with thousands of dead or dying Frenchmen. Will was filled with mixed emotions: he was proud of the fact that his king had won, but at the same time he felt sickened by all the death around him. Surely there must be other ways to settle disputes, no matter how important they were. But he knew it was not for him, a lowly illbred archer, to question the wisdom or demands of his king. But inside it still troubled Will. And he knew after today, he would never quite feel the same about war; and that after this campaign, if he were fortunate enough to still be alive, he would try never to kill anyone again.

On the battlefield where the Constable had fallen, King Henry asked a captured French knight for the name of the castle that could be seen above the nearby treetops.

"Azincourt, my lord," the knight replied. Although he spoke in English, his accent made the name sound like "Agincourt."

"Then," King Henry said, "as all battles should bear the name of the castle nearest to where they occur, this shall for ever be called the Battle of Agincourt."

Hardly noticed among the many treasures that the Portuguese nobleman Pedro Alvares Cabral presented to his king, Manuel 1, on his return from his voyage to the Far East, were a bow and some arrows.

They were unlike any bow and arrows ever seen by the nobles of the Portuguese court, and when Cabral explained he had taken them from the savages who inhabited the newly discovered Portuguese territory known as "Terra da Cruz," the primitive weapons were examined with mild curiosity. Then, everyone's attention returned to the silks and spices and other treasures obtained in trading with Far Eastern rulers, and the discarded bow and arrows were left to gather dust in a castle storeroom.

THE PORTUGUESE

IN EARLY MARCH, A.D. 1500, Pedro Alvares Cabral, a Portuguese nobleman whose father, Fernao, was a favorite at court, set sail from Lisbon in command of thirteen ships. His own vessel, the *Pedraluiz*, an 80-foot caravel whose lateen mainsail bore the family crest, proudly led the fleet out of the harbor.

Cabral was an imposing, strikingly handsome man of thirty-two with shoulder-length dark hair, full beard, and a flashing smile, who was well-known for his elegant manners and persuasive, impetuous charm. His mission was to inaugurate trade with the Far East, and such was the importance of the occasion that King Manuel 1 himself, the man responsible for selecting Cabral as the commander over many other more accomplished sailors, was at dockside to see the young nobleman off.

Manuel I was a wise monarch, who hoped Cabral's persuasive powers would serve him well in trading matters; but the king also knew the fleet first had to reach its destination, the important seaport of Calicut in Madras Province, India, and to compensate for Cabral's lack of sailing experience Manuel I appointed Bartolomes Diaz, a veteran navigator who was the first European to round the Cape of Good Hope, as second in command. Spain and Italy were also interested in trading with the Far East, and Cabral's orders were to reach Calicut as quickly as possible. He passed these orders onto Diaz, who knew the trade routes as well as any man. The canny navigator, in an effort to avoid being becalmed off the traditionally windless coast of Africa, plotted a course that was far west of the normal route and the fleet headed out into the Atlantic Ocean.

Winds were good, and all went well for the first ten days at sea. Then, the fleet ran into a series of mid-Atlantic storms. Gales and high seas buffeted the thirteen vessels off-course, blowing them so far west that on April 22, six weeks after leaving Lisbon, a lookout on Cabral's ship sighted a strange, new coastline.

Cabral officially logged the sighting, and ordered his scrivener, Pero Vaz de Caminha, to record all the events that followed. Then, anchoring in a small jungle-fringed cove, Cabral went ashore with a party of armed men.

Uppermost in his mind was the 1494 Treaty of Tordesillas, in which the Spanish and Portuguese crowns agreed to divide the world—Spain taking the west, Portugal the east. The two monarchs, ignorant of modern geography, accepted a demarcating line that gave the eastern coast of South America to Portugal. Hence, after studying his maps, Cabral knew he was within his legal rights to claim this new discovery for his country and after much careful thought and a discussion with his Catholic advisors, he named it "Terra da Cruz" or Land of the True Cross. Inland, beyond the narrow strip of sandy beach, the vine-tangled jungle was so dense, so infested with snakes and mosquitoes, Cabral chose not to attempt any major exploration. But since some of his men had glimpsed several swarthy, long-haired, naked Indians watching them curiously from the thick foliage, Cabral decided to try and make contact with them.

He brought ashore his Franciscan friars, who were aboard especially for the purpose of coverting non-believers into Christians, and had his men set out hand-mirrors, lengths of rope, and a few bolts of gayly colored cloth invitingly on the beach.

The Portuguese waited patiently, but nothing happened. The strangely painted faces continued to watch them curiously from the safety of the jungle, but not one of the Indians ventured onto the beach.

Finally, as nightfall approached, the friars suggested that they leave the gifts and return to the ship. Hoping the Indians would take this as a show of good faith, Cabral agreed. He and the landing party got into the boats and rowed back to the *Pedraluiz*. There, on board the high narrow poop deck, Cabral watched through his spyglass as presently the Indians emerged from the jungle and cautiously approached the pile of gifts.

The Indians were members of the Tupinamba tribe, who lived and hunted along the Atlantic coast. They were all men of medium height, well-muscled, and naked save for a wide belt made of bark that they wore around their middle. They had flat faces with high cheekbones, dark inquisitive eyes, broad noses and wide, thick-lipped mouths. Some had pierced their lower lips and wore bone ornaments in them. A few had feathers woven into their long, unkempt black hair, while others wore feather armlets and had painted their faces and bodies with red and yellow juices from vegetable roots. Most were armed with bows and arrows, but two of the larger men also carried clubs and spears with brightly painted bone points.

The Indians examined the gifts with great caution, as if suspecting some kind of trap; then, when no harm came to them, they grew less afraid and began talking excitedly among themselves and pointing at the Portuguese fleet.

After several minutes their chief, Ucayli, a stocky, big-chested man in his early forties, held up his hands for silence. He then spoke animatedly for a moment, and gestured inland. Two of the men put down their bows and arrows and ran into the jungle. They returned shortly, carrying armfuls of fruit which they placed in a pile on the sand near the gifts. Then, Ucayli raised his bow and arrows in salute to the Portuguese ships anchored offshore, turned, and led his tribe off into the jungle.

Next morning Cabral, the friars and a party of armed men returned to the beach. Crabs and insects had eaten much of the fruit, but a few untouched mangoes tasted delicious to the fruit-starved sailors. As they sat there, eating, Cabral and the others pretended not to notice the Indians watching them from the jungle.

"Let them think we don't care about them," Cabral told his men. "Then, perhaps, they'll lose their fear of us and come out into the open."

It took several hours, but finally Chief Ucayli and a few of the bravest Indians left the jungle and, bows and arrows in hand, timidly approached the Portuguese.

Cabral and the friars greeted the Indians, and with the help of sign language tried to explain who they were and where they had come from. Behind them, the sailors held their muskets at the ready, prepared to shoot if the Indians showed any signs of aggression.

The sailors need not have worried. Following Chief Ucayli's example, the primitive Tupinambas were friendly, curious, and very much in awe of the white-skinned strangers. They had obviously never seen a white man before and were especially awed by one of the friars who had red hair, and by a sailor whose blond beard and long hair were bleached white by the sun.

After both sides had grown more at ease with each other, Cabral invited Ucayli and his men on board the *Pedraluiz*. The chief accepted, but refused to get into the rowboats until his men had gone into the jungle and from their hidden village acquired several tame parrots and small, bewhiskered monkeys.

The Indians explained through sign language that they wanted to trade the animals for gifts, and once on board the caravel Cabral gave them sheets of paper and bolts of cloth. Delighted, Chief Ucayli presented Cabral with his bow and arrows. He also showed the Portuguese nobleman how to shoot, and at Cabral's request demonstrated how accurate the primitive weapon was by constantly hitting a small mark made on the mainmast.

The bow was beautifully made of palmwood, over six feet in length with long tapering limbs, and had no handle section or wrapping to denote where to hold it. The wood had been smoothed to a silklike finish with sandstone, and each limb was partly covered with thin fiber binding and decorated with brightly colored macaw feathers. The same thin fiber, taken from palm tree leaves, was rolled and twisted together to make the bowstring.

The reed arrows were almost as long as the bow, had hardwood foreshafts and long bone points that were painted with decorative patterns. The arrows were fletched with two macaw feathers—bound to the shaft with vegetable fiber—and each shaft had a notch cut at the back end that was wrapped with fiber to prevent splitting.

After the Indian chief stopped shooting, Cabral decided to put on a demonstration of his own firepower. Ordering an empty wine keg thrown overboard, Cabral had his musketeers pepper it with shots. He then told his master gunner to blow it out of the water with a single cannon ball.

The Tupinambas had never seen firearms before. They were alarmed by the musket fire, and so terrified by the cannon shot that they threw themselves cowering on the deck. Amused, Cabral and the friars helped the frightened Indians to their feet, and tried to calm them with food and water.

Later, the Indians were taken ashore. There, Cabral forced them to reveal the whereabouts of their village—a cluster of small crude palmwood huts in a jungle clearing two hundred yards from the beach. Naked women and children greeted the Portuguese, showing the same timid curiosity and awe that the Indian men had displayed previously.

Cabral, hoping to find gold or precious stones, was greatly disappointed by the impoverished conditions and after a thorough search ordered his men back to the ship. There, in his cabin, Cabral gave orders to his 2nd-in-command, Diaz, to be ready to sail on the dawn tide.

The next morning, two hours before dawn, a force of armed sailors went ashore and attacked the Tupinamba village. The Indians were still asleep and were captured without a shot being fired. The Portuguese broke their bows and spears, put the strongest of the young men in shackles and, ignoring Chief Ucayli's pleas, took them back to the *Pedraluiz*. There, they were locked in the hold where they would remain until the fleet reached Calicut and they could be sold as slaves.

Dawn came and the Portuguese fleet pulled out of the cove. Aboard the *Pedraluiz*, in his small but plushly appointed cabin, Pedro Alvares Cabral toyed with the bow and arrows given to him by Chief Ucayli and reflected upon the great honor and fame he would receive when he returned to Portugal and presented this savage new land to his king.

While on the beach, the Tupinambas sadly watched the ships sail away, their hearts broken by the loss of their young men.

The Turks were the finest bowyers ever to grace this earth. Their beautiful, composite, recurve bows often took two or three years to make, but when they were finished and ready to shoot, they out-performed any bow in history.

THE TURKS

IN CONSTANTINOPLE it was the day of Chidr-Ilyas, the Great Spring Festival of the Orient. This meant it was also the start of the archery season. Every archer belonging to the Archery Guild rode out to the suburbs and gathered on the ok meidan, a vast field on a level hilltop overlooking the city and the harbor that was designated for the purpose of archery.

The Archery Guild had been formed in 1453, shortly after Constantinople was conquered by the Turks; within a few months Mohammed II, an avid archer, established the ok meidan. He established it by a decree, so that no one could ever convert the field into burial grounds or botanical gardens. Years later, during the reign of Bayezid II, the archery enthusiast Iskender Pasha donated a guild house and a mosque in which religious services were performed before each archery tournament.

Now, on this sunny blue day in 1798, services had just been completed and a huge crowd waited on the sidelines to watch the great sultan, Selim III, officially open the tournament by shooting the first arrow.

The Sultan, a very complex young man who preferred the company of men to that of women, was standing outside his tent with his retinue, talking to foreign dignitaries.

One of these was the British Ambassador, Sir Robert Ainslie, a reserved, distinguished gentleman who shared the Sultan's great interest in archery. He was at the tournament, in fact, because Selim had promised that today he would eclipse the record for distance shooting. The present record of 1281 1/2 pikes (890 yards) was held by the famous Ottoman champion, Toz Koparan, and displayed on a marble marker erected on the spot where the arrow had fallen. Other marble columns denoting former records also stood on the field, but they'd all been established many years ago and the big crowd was excitedly waiting for their beloved Sultan to make history in front of them.

Selim was a handsome young man, despite slight traces of childhood smallpox on his fair skin. He was of medium height, with dark blond hair and a beard that was artifically darkened. He was muscular and, like most Ottomans, short-legged. But he presented an impressive picture in his scarlet robes, elaborate white turban held by a diamond brooch and crested with a white egret plume. His tunic was gold and blue, his silk pantaloons rose-colored, his shoes pale yellow. Now, as he took up his powerful, short composite horn-and-sinew bow and pulled it a few times to flex his muscles, the crowd cheered loudly and stamped their feet in anticipation. Sultan Selim waved graciously to them, and continued warming up with the bow.

It was his favorite bow, weighing a little more than one hundred pounds. The core was made of maple wood from the vicinity of Kastamuni, with strips of pure black horn of the carabao, or water buffalo, glued onto the belly and several layers of cow tendons glued to the back. A special decorative lacquer had then been applied to the finished bow, after which it was rubbed with sandlewood oil until it gleamed like dark burnished gold.

With his muscles now warmed up, Sultan Selim was ready to shoot. He looked at the sheik-ul-meidan, who was testing the wind with a towel. The Field Master held the towel up by its upper corners, watching carefully as it swayed gently, as a whole, and not in waves. Conditions were favorable, with the wind blowing out of the east—as it had done for all of the prior records—and the satisfied Field Master nodded respectfully to the Sultan.

"Shoot, O Mighty Sultan," he said quietly. "And may Allah give you strength."

Selim solemnly faced west and drew a flight arrow from his golden quiver. On the wrist of his bow-hand was the *siper*, or arrow guide. The small oval shooting plate, with its leather-covered ivory groove in which the arrow rested as it is drawn back into the bow, was fastened by a leather strap to the Sultan's left hand. Its purpose was so flight shooters could draw a short arrow several inches inside the bow, and that, upon release, the arrow would be guided safely past the bow hand.

All the Sultan's flight arrows measured 24.45 inches. They were made of pine, barreled, with both ends tapered and with a bone tip and a tiny nock made of brazil wood. Three small feathers were glued on immediately ahead of the nock, each feather taken from the left wing of a swan. The arrows took days to cut and to shape and were made only by the guild of arrow makers. These perfectionists selected only trees that were ten years old, or older, and cut them only during their period of dormancy. Billets, two digits square, were stored outside for two months to air-dry, then stacked in a baking oven and held at exactly the temperature that master arrow makers had found from vast experience to be ideal. After being in the oven long enough for the pitch and rosin to have oozed out of them, the billets were stored in a well-ventilated, dry room for three to five years. Then, and only then, would a master arrow maker's conscience allow him to consider making them into arrow shafts.

The Sultan, well aware of the meticulous care taken to make his arrows, carefully nocked his arrow on his unspun silk bowstring, made sure the shaft lay correctly in the *siper* groove, hooked his ivory thumb ring over the string and extended his up-angled bow arm toward the far end of the field. He then slowly and smoothly pulled the arrow back until the point was

"Shoot, O Mighty Sultan."

level with the belly of the bow. Then, after a slight pause, he continued pulling with a sudden, violent jerk until the arrow was resting in the *siper* groove and his draw-hand reached his right ear. At that instant, Selim released the arrow. The final pull and release were done so swiftly, none of the spectators actually saw the arrow at full draw and most assumed the Sultan hadn't completed the shot.

But the archers knew better. Sultan Selim had perfected this art of releasing, called "snap-shooting," and with it could shoot arrows farther than any of his competitors.

The arrow arced high into the sunlight and seemed to fly out of sight. Finally, it landed in the grass near the end of the field. Everyone gasped, for the arrow was almost one hundred paces beyond the marble marker bearing Toz Koparan's previous record.

"My God!" exclaimed Sir Robert Ainslie as the clamoring of the crowd swelled all around him. "If I hadn't been here, I never would've believed that such a shot was possible!"

When carefully measured by the Field Master, using a marker cord, the distance of Selim's shot was an incredible 1400 pikes, or 972 yards and 2 3/4 inches!

The crowd roared its approval. The Sultan's retinue, and all the foreign dignitaries, gathered around the Sultan to congratulate him on his remarkable shot. Selim was quietly pleased. He praised Allah for assisting him, and modestly suggested that the wind must have been extra strong today.

But no one was listening. They had witnessed a record that they knew would exist for a very long time, if not forever, and wanted no one, not even their beloved Sultan, to belittle its importance.

With the event of gunpowder and bullets, the bow as a weapon of war steadily declined over the centuries. Eventually, the British love of the longbow turned archery into a sporting event that, up until the end of the nineteenth century, was still barely known throughout the United States.

Indirectly, that was all changed by the result of the Civil War and by the initiative of two "Southerners" who were forced to live by "Yankee" laws.

THE SOUTHERNERS

THE REVIVAL OF archery in the United States rests solely upon the shoulders of the Thompson brothers, Maurice and Will, who were born and raised in the hill country of northern Georgia. As boys they played Robin Hood, using crudely made bows and arrows, and hunted small game and birds in the woods surrounding the family plantation.

Originally self-taught, in their teens they became acquainted with an old hermit who lived in the woods bordering their father's plantation. His name was Thomas Williams, and although his reclusive nature stopped him from demonstrating his archery skills in public, the old man could shoot with incredible accuracy.

Seeing the boys' love of archery, and how inadequate their skills with a bow and arrow were, the humble, soft-spoken, bearded hermit overcame his shyness long enough to teach Maurice and Will the correct way to shoot. It took many weeks of long, diligent practice but finally both boys could hit most creatures with their first arrow, whether it was moving or motionless. Combined with their already excellent tracking techniques and knowledge of animal behavior in the woods, the Thompson brothers soon became expert hunters.

How long Maurice and Will would have continued their love affair with archery is impossible to know. Perhaps under normal circumstances, as they entered manhood, earning a living or getting married and raising a family might have taken precedence and forced them to forget archery or, at best, to treat it only as a minor hobby. If that had been the case, archery might have remained a past-time enjoyed only by the English who, even then, in the 1860s, knew the pleasure of shooting at targets.

But Fate intervened in the shape of the Civil War. Maurice and Will joined the Confederate army and marched away to fight against the Union troops.

Both brothers fought bravely, and distinguished themselves in several skirmishes with the enemy. Then, in June, 1864, during the battle of Cold Harbor, Maurice, the older by four years, was shot in the chest and severely wounded. He was released from hospital before he had fully recouperated, but, typically, didn't complain and bravely remained in the thick of the fighting until the end of the war.

When peace was declared a year later, Maurice was still weak and needed his brother to help him get back home to Georgia. It was a long, painful journey that ended in near-despair when the brothers found their plantation had been burned to the ground by Union soldiers. Crushed, and with no means of immediately making a living, the brothers decided to live in the neighboring hills and woods. There, they hunted game for food, and forbidden by the Union laws to use firearms, they returned to the weapon they had both learned to shoot so proficiently as youngsters: the bow and arrow.

They lived in the hills and woods for almost two years. Then Maurice, whose lung would never completely heal, became sick with the approach of a second winter. After a long serious discussion, he and Will agreed that they should spend the winter months in a warmer climate. So, in autumn, they left the hills of northern Georgia and headed south toward Florida.

Before reaching their destination, Jacksonville, the brothers spent a month hunting in the Okefinokee Swamp. This was their first visit to the southeastern part of the state and in the tiny town of Magnolia, located on the edge of the great swamp, they listened, fascinated, as the local old timers spun fanciful tales about events that had made the area famous.

The Thompsons learned how in the early and mid-eighteen hundreds the indomitable Seminoles had retreated into the depths of the swamp, refusing to surrender and fighting off the military might of the United States for years; how deserters from the Confederate armies had vanished into the dense, chartless swampland and were never seen again; and how, near the end of the Civil War, countless runaway slaves had hidden in the impenetrable swamp, remaining in their sanctury until the Union army was finally victorious and they were liberated.

The Thompsons also learned that presently there were few if any humans living in the swamp, and that the nearly seven hundred square miles of vine-tangled, grass-choked, cypress-studded shallow water was teeming with wildlife. It was an invitation they couldn't refuse. Hiring a young, recently freed slave, Jordan Wilson, to guide them, Maurice and Will purchased two ancient dugout canoes, some necessary provisions and paddled into the swamp.

"Jord," as he was commonly called, had been one of the runaway slaves who had taken refuge in the Okefinokee and knew the swamp better than anyone. For fifty cents a day, plus meals, he guided the brothers into areas never before seen by a white man, giving them opportunities to hunt and fish in an unspoiled natural paradise.

The Thompsons spent almost four weeks in the Okefinokee. Then, saying goodbye to Jord, they headed south to Florida. In Jacksonville, they sold several heron skins and otter pelts and with the money purchased a small, makeshift sailboat, provisions and a trained hound dog named Skeeter. They also hired another former slave, Caesar, to guide them down the St. Johns' river and along its innumerable tributaries and backwaters. Here they spent the winter hunting, fishing and relaxing in the warm, humid temperatures.

The winter passed quickly, and as spring approached Maurice and Will returned to their beloved hills in northern Georgia. But the mild weather had done wonders for Maurice's health, and both brothers agreed that from now on they would return to Florida every autumn and spend the winter exploring new regions to hunt and fish.

In the seventies the Thompsons moved to Crawfordsville, Indiana. There, Maurice turned his piles of meticulous notes on their hunting experiences into articles and stories that were published in national magazines. They were so well-received that in 1877 the best of these stories were gathered together and made into a book called "The Witchery of Archery."

The book's unique charm and instant popularity brought archery to the public's attention. Archery clubs were formed about the country, and in 1878 several archery enthusiasts from Chicago visited the Thompsons in Crawfordsville with the purpose of organizing the scattered clubs into the National Archery Association, electing Maurice as the first president.

The following year in August the first N.A.A. championship tournament was held in Chicago, and, not surprisingly, Will was the winner.

The Thompsons continued shooting for the remainder of their lives. And although the ever-frail Maurice never attained the tournament victories achieved by his younger, healthier brother, his numerous writings about both bow-hunting and target archery more than compensated for his lower scores.

Few people were more dependent, spiritually or physically, upon the bow and arrow than the American Indian. Even when they were introduced to firearms, most tribes did not give up the bow and arrow as an essential weapon.

As Geronimo once stated: "The spirit of the bow dwells in the heart of all young men..."

THE APACHES

THE OLD MAN sat hunched-over on a hard-backed chair outside his small, wooden house, his eyesight failing but his fingers still deft enough to use a knife to shape the limbs of the bow he was making.

He did not resemble the tall, proud, regal-looking Indians that Catlin or Remington painted. Age had shrunken his once-sturdy frame, his copper-colored skin was terribly wrinkled, and his long black hair heavily streaked with silver. Dressed in white man's clothes, he wore an old straw hat with an upturned brim that was adorned with two eagle feathers, a tobacco-stained red bandanna, a worn brown vest buttoned over a blue-striped shirt that was tucked into faded Levi's, and badly scuffed shoes: a once-bloodthirsty warrior who had outlived his time, and who now looked sad, undignified and defeated.

Gone was the defiant, haughty look in his eyes; gone was the fierce, menacing scowl; and, sadly, gone was the wild indomitable spirit that enabled him to elude 5,000 U.S. troopers led by

Generals Crook and Miles and remain a hunted renegade, leading his ragtag band of outlaw Chiricahaus on raids out of Mexico into Texas, New Mexico and Arizona, terrifying ranchers and settlers for over a decade.

Now, on this hot dusty summer day in 1908, the Apache whose Indian name was Goyahkla (One Who Yawns), but whom white men knew only as Geronimo, was just a weary, dispirited man of seventy-nine who earned a few dollars selling autographed photographs of himself in outlandish costumes that no true Apache brave would have been caught dead in!

He also sold copies of his book, "Geronimo's Story of His Life," an autobiography that he had dictated through a translator to S.M. Barrett several years ago, along with bows and arrows and beaded, buckskin quivers and distinctive, knee-high Apache boots that he made and, for an extra fifty cents, would sign with his carefully printed name:

G E R O N I M O.

Earlier, knowing that tourists would come around later, he had spread out all his goods on a soiled Indian blanket on the hot sun-baked dirt before him, and was now just making another bow while he waited for them to arrive.

Finished shaping the limbs, he held up the bow and examined its symmetry with his weak but well-trained eyes. Thanks to the Great White Chief in Washington, who forced him to live on the Ft. Sill reservation many hundreds of miles from his beloved Chiricahua mountains in Arizona, he had become a mere caricature of his once-fearsome self. But outward appearances had nothing to do with his inner self; his pride in his ability, as an Indian artisan, to make a bow he was proud of and could sell to the white eyes with respect.

As with most Indians, the bow and arrow were part of his heritage. Long before the arrival of the white man's rifle or pistol, he and the other young braves had hunted with the bow and, when at war, used it to kill their enemies.

Now, looking at the unfinished bow, Geronimo let his mind wander back through time to the distant, clouded past when he was a child and his father, Taklishim (The Gray One), the son of Chief Mahko of the Bedonkohe tribe, had taught him the art of bow-making. That was in the late 1820s and early '30s, when the Bedonkohes were a separate tribe of Apaches who lived in the mountains and canyons just north of the true Chiricahuas. But as Geronimo grew up, and his father died, the matter of survival and much intermarrying caused the Bedonkohes to lose their identity and to become known as, simply, Chiricahuas.

It was on his fifth birthday, Geronimo remembered, when his father took him aside and told him that the day had come for Goyahkla to learn how to make a bow and arrow. The boy's heart swelled with pride. For though the Apaches' arsenal of weapons included the lance, stone-headed warclub, and rawhide sling, the weapon they most relied on was a short, powerful bow that had a lethal range of 100 yards.

Heart pounding with excitment, Goyahkla watched in silence as his father selected one of the many ash staves he kept drying in a corner of their wickiup, and then shaped it with his knife until he was satisfied with the flat, tapered limbs and slightly rounded handle section. The chief next held the bow in the smoke of the fire, gently bending the limbs over a warm stone with his hands until they were curved to his satisfaction. It took much time, patience and skill, and Goyahkla could barely control his excitement as he watched and waited, silently squatted beside his father, his eyes smarting from the upcurling smoke.

While the bow was being prepared, Goyahkla's sister, Nahdos-te, chewed several lengths of animal sinew until they were soft and pliable. Outside the wickiup, her mother boiled fish skins in a small pot until they melted and became glue.

When the glue was the right texture, Chief Taklishim glued the sinew to the back of the bow to add resilience to the wood, and then additionally secured each strip with rawhide wrappings. Lastly, while the glue dried, he showed his son how to make a bowstring by twisting together two lengths of sinew and making a loop at one end, which could be looped over the tip of the upper limb while the other end was tied around the tip of the bottom limb.

It was now time to learn how to make arrows. The chief took down a bundle of reeds that he kept stored in the roof of his wickiup, and began selecting the straightest ones for his son's arrows. The Apaches called the reed "*klo-ka,*" or arrow grass, and considered it the best material for arrows as it needed very little straightening.

While the men were preparing the arrows, Goyahkla's mother and sister sewed together pieces of deerskin to make him a bow case and a quiver. They added beads and leather fringes as decoration, and burned his name on the deerskin with a hot ember.

Meanwhile, Chief Taklishim showed his son how to cut a small notch at the end of each arrow, wide enough for the bowstring to fit snugly, and to then bind the shaft just below the notch to prevent further splitting. Next, pieces of obsidian were chipped into the shape of arrowheads that were slotted into the front end of the arrows and then bound with sinew to prevent slippage.

Finally, three hawk feathers were trimmed and tied to the nock-end of each shaft. The arrows were now ready to shoot, and young Goyahkla eagerly accompanied his father to a nearby canyon where small game abounded.

Now, recalling those wonderful moments in his distant past, Geronimo smiled and saw in his mind fleeting images of darting rabbits, deer bounding over rocks, and arrows winging their way toward their elusive, fleeing targets. Then, suddenly, the memories of hunting animals were blotted out by another, more startling image—that of two prospectors, panning the riverbed for gold—and Geronimo was jolted back to reality.

They were the first whites he had ever seen. And as he sat there in the blazing hot Oklahoma sun, remembering the momentous occasion, Geronimo recalled how curious and wary he had been of the two bearded, pale-skinned strangers. His father showed no fear of the prospectors, but neither did he seem inclined to make his or Goyahkla's presence known to them. Instead, father and son remained crouched behind some rocks overlooking the Gila River, watching the two grizzled, weatherbeaten white men dipping their pans into the water.

"What are they doing, my father?"

"Looking for a strange yellow metal that is valuable to them," Chief Taklishim replied. "They call it gold."

"Are we going to kill them, like we kill Mexicans?" Goyahkla asked.

"No, my son. We are at war with the slave-catchers; we are not at war with the whites." And so, after quietly watching the prospectors for awhile, Goyahkla and his father returned to camp to alert everyone that white men were in the area.

Geronimo's thoughts were suddenly interrupted by the sound of voices approaching. He looked up, his watery red-rimmed eyes squinting in the bright sunlight, and saw three people walking toward his property. One he recognized as Lieutenant Purington, an officer from the fort. The other two were strangers: a tall, fleshy-faced, middle-aged man with a big flowing mustache, and a boy of eight, who had red curly hair, blue eyes and a shy smile. Geronimo, having visited St. Louis and Washington, D.C., guessed the newcomers were easterners by the cut of their clothing.

He watched them come along the path that ran beside the wire fence enclosing his property, and pause outside the wooden gate.

"Buenos dias, Jefe. "Lt. Purington saluted Geronimo respectfully, then added in Spanish: "Are we welcome in your house?"

Geronimo liked the young officer and immediately signaled for Lt. Purington to enter. He did, holding the gate open for the visitors and then leading the way up to Geronimo. As they walked, the boy lagged timidly behind his father, eyes saucers, his expression filled with a mixture of awe and uncertainty.

"Does he speak English, lieutenant?" the man asked as they approached Geronimo.

"Enough to hawk his wares," Lt. Purington said. "But he prefers Apache or Spanish."

The three stopped before Geronimo, who rose and greeted them. Lt. Purington introduced everybody, and explained to Geronimo that Mr. Monroe and his son, Jason, were visiting from Baltimore. The old Indian proudly replied that he knew of this Baltimore, because the Great White Chief Roosevelt had spoken of it during Geronimo's visit to the capital for the President's inauguration.

While the adults were talking, Jason lost some of his timidness

Geronimo suddenly held his hand up.

as he saw the bows and arrows that lay on the blanket among the other souvenirs. He had always wanted a bow and arrow, and now asked his father to buy them for him. Mr. Monroe wasn't too thrilled by the idea. Baltimore was a civilized city, and the thought of his son shooting someone, even by accident, set him against the purchase. Even Jason's promise never to shoot the bow at anyone, or in a public area, failed to alter Mr. Monroe's mind.

Geronimo, who had remained silent as father and son debated, suddenly held his hand up and said: "Geronimo, him speak."

Mr. Monroe and his son turned to the old warrior.

"What is it, Chief?" Lt. Purington asked him in Spanish.

"The spirit of the bow dwells in the heart of all young men," Geronimo said solemnly. "It is not wise for a father to crush that spirit, any more than it would be for an eagle to tell his young not to fly."

"What did he say?" Mr. Monroe asked Lt. Purington.

The officer repeated Geronimo's statement. The words seemed to affect Mr. Monroe, jogging his memory, drawing his eyebrows together in a deep frown as he mulled things over.

"Didn't you ever want to shoot a bow and arrow?" Jason said, sensing his father was wavering.

Mr. Monroe thought for another moment, then slowly nodded. "Many times," he admitted. He rested his hand fondly on his son's head and ruffled his curly red hair. "But my father would never allow such a 'heathen' weapon in the house." He smiled, as if amused by the recollection, then turned to Geronimo, adding: "Your point is well taken, Chief." Then to his son: "Pick out the bow you like. And one of those quivers to hold your arrows."

After his visitors had left, Geronimo sat there in the hot sun, dozing, lost in thought, until he fell asleep. And while he slept, he dreamed he was a boy again, wild and free as the wind, hunting the deer and the fox and the rabbit among the canyons and mountains of his beloved Arizona.

James "Doug" Easton became interested in archery literally by accident. But his interest soon turned into an obsession. And in the ensuing years, he made archery tackle for many of the finest archers in the world.

Although Doug did not invent the aluminum arrow, he, more than anyone, saw its potential and through hard work, ingenuity, and plain determination, did his best to create the perfect arrow.

THE ARROW MAKER

IT WAS EARLY in the summer of 1922 when the tall, slender young man parked his old car at the edge of the park. Getting out, he removed his archery tackle from the trunk and headed toward the range. He walked with a definite limp. He had only discarded his crutches a few days ago, and it was obvious just walking on his left leg caused him a certain amount of pain. But he seemed determined to ignore the discomfort, and limped across the broad grassy archery range toward a small group of white-clad archers who were practicing on the shooting line.

He was a shy young man, barely turned eighteen, and this was the first time he had ever shot a bow and arrow in public. But the members of the Oakland Archery Club quickly welcomed him to their weekly shoot, and after being introduced around he felt less nervous and conspicuous in their midst. He paid the small fee required to shoot in the tournament, signed the register "Doug Easton," and joined the other archers on the shooting line. After he'd shot a few ends, Doug was approached by an older man who wasn't shooting but whom everyone knew and treated with great respect. The man, who stood athletically erect and wore casual but expensive clothes, stopped a few paces away and watched Doug shoot.

It was obvious he admired Doug's bow, but he politely made no attempt to speak or interrupt him until he'd shot his last arrow at the target. Then, in a soft, cultured voice, he asked Doug where he'd gotten such a beautiful bow.

"I made it," Doug said.

The older man looked impressed. "Where'd you learn such fine craftsmanship?"

"From a book," Doug explained. "I read it over and over while I was in hospital, recuperating from a shotgun accident. Then, when I got home a few weeks ago, I couldn't wait to make a bow."

"This is your *first* bow?" the man said, even more impressed. "Good heavens, that's incredible. And what was the name of this book?" he added.

"Hunting with the Bow and Arrow," Doug replied. "By Dr. Saxton Pope."

The older man looked at Doug, long and hard. Then he smiled wryly, offered Doug his hand and said: "Young man— I'm Dr. Pope."

Doug couldn't believe his ears; or his good luck. Dr. Pope and his close friend, Art Young, were responsible for the revival of bow-and-arrow hunting, a sport that had lain dormant ever since the initial public response to the writings and hunting exploits of the Thompson brothers had died down. Thanks to Pope and Young, who had successfully hunted big game animals all over North America, as well as in other parts of the world, numerous archers and gun-hunters were now turning to the challenging sport of bowhunting.

Barely able to keep calm, Doug had countless questions for Dr. Pope. The older man patiently answered every one of them, and the two men continued discussing the art of bow-making, and archery in general, for over an hour. Doug explained that he had read numerous other archery books while recuperating, and that archery had become almost an obsession with him.

He loved to shoot and to make bows and arrows, and hoped that one day he could open an archery shop and make a living at the sport. Dr. Pope felt exactly as Doug did about archery, especially when it concerned hunting, and explained that he had been hooked by the sport ever since he'd befriended the Indian, Ishi.

Doug knew the name well, for Dr. Pope had gone into great detail in his book to describe his close relationship with the primitive American Indian who, in 1911, as the last survivor of the Yana tribe, was forced by starvation to leave the wilderness around Mount Lassen and expose himself to the white settlers living on the outskirts of Oroville, California.

When the news of the last wild Indian hit the newspapers, Professor T.T. Watterman, of the Department of Anthropology at the University of California, was dispatched to examine the man.

The Indian was being held in the local jail for his own safekeeping. He was terrified of his white captors, expecting them to kill him, and had refused to drink or eat any of the food they had given him. Professor Watterman tried to converse with the Indian in a variety of tribal dialects, none of which the man understood. Finally, the professor used a word from the Yana language, and instantly broke through the impasse. The Indian began to speak, trusting Professor Watterman and treating him as a friend. He explained that his name was Ishi, and that his tribe had been wiped out by white men several years ago. Since then he had been hiding in the dense brush and volcanic rocks of Deer Creek Canyon, trying to survive without betraying his presence to his white enemies. But game had become scarce, and faced with starvation Ishi had sneaked into the outskirts of Oroville early one morning in hopes of finding food. Instead, a barking dog had cornered him in a corral and Ishi, too weak to escape, had been captured by the town policeman.

Impressed by the Indian's honesty, and thrilled by the idea of being able to study an unspoiled, living example of the Stone Age, Professor Watterman took him back to San Francisco. Ishi was given a place to live at the Museum of Anthropology, where he lived happily, working as a janitor and becoming a favorite with the staff for five years. Then, susceptible to the white man's diseases, Ishi contacted tuberculosis and, despite all the medication and efforts of the medical staff, he died shortly thereafter.

During those five years, though, Ishi was befriended by Dr. Pope, who became an instructor in surgery at the University Medical School—and it was through their warm association and numerous hunting trips in the field together, that Dr. Pope got hooked on archery.

Remembering all these things, Doug now asked Dr. Pope if he knew of anyone who might hire him to make their archery tackle. Dr. Pope thought a moment, then recommended Doug call a company in Oakland called "California By-Products," who had an archery division. Doug thanked the quiet, unassuming surgeon, the two men shook hands, then Doug limped to the target to collect his arrows.

It was the only time Doug ever met Dr. Pope; but their chance meeting greatly influenced young Easton's future...and eventually gave the archery world the aluminum arrow.

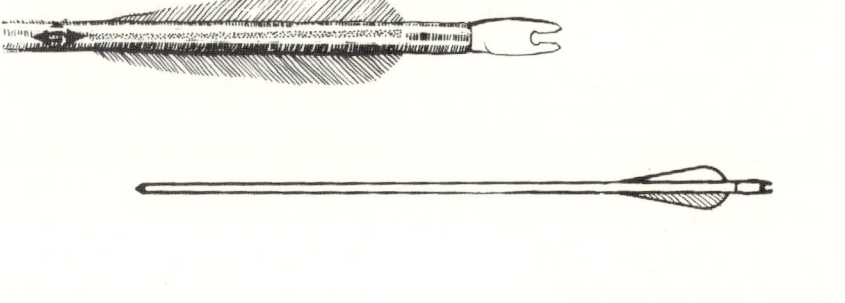

Dr. Saxton Pope and Art Young did much in the 1920s and '30s to bring archery to the attention of the public. But despite their wonderful skills and hunting exploits, they were not able to popularize it—make it a sport that appealed to the masses.

That task fell to one man and one man only: Howard Hill.

THE ARCHER

THANKS TO THE FAME and popularity of the guest speaker, the auditorium adjoining a church in Encino, California, was packed. Row after row of Boy Scouts in neatly pressed uniforms sat in front of the small raised stage, their fresh youthful faces aglow with excitment.

Behind the scouts sat their parents and friends, along with a select group of archery enthusiasts who were looking forward to tonight's demonstration and collection of amusing, enthralling anecdotes as much as the eager youngsters.

For on this summer night in 1960, they were privileged to enjoy the company of a very special man, someone who had done more to bring archery to the attention of the general public than any other: the legendary Howard Hill.

Reflecting upon his innumerable feats, accomplishments, world records and longevity in the sport, young Steve found it difficult not to be in awe of the man. For Howard Hill had reached the exalted position in archery that was comparable to

Babe Ruth in baseball, Johnny Unitas in football, Pele in soccer, Joe Louis in boxing, and all the other great athletes who have so dominated their sport that their name has become synonymous with it.

Yet, when Howard met someone, he made it impossible for that person to be in awe of him by displaying such warmth, homespun charisma, and a genuine interest in them, as a person, that they immediately felt as if they had known the man since childhood.

Everyone sensed at once that he was down-to-earth, someone to hunt with, swap stories with, the friend they'd like to have, flamboyant perhaps but always decent and unselfish—as tonight readily proved. For Howard, through a mixup of dates, was asked to speak at a businessmen's dinner for which he would have been paid several thousand dollars. But, having already promised to give a demonstration to the Boy Scouts—for free—Howard didn't even hesitate about which choice to make.

"Young'ns always come first, brother, no matter what," he told young Steve. "Now, what time d'you want ol' Pappy to show up?"

Steve watched him now as he came out on the stage, a big, burly, powerful man whose erect carriage, youthful energy and thick black hair belied his sixty-one years. He cut off Steve's glowing introduction with a casual "All right, partner, they've heard enough," and instantly captured the audience's attention with a humorous anecdote about bear hunting with an old friend named Jimbo.

"Well, folks, one mornin' ol' Jimbo, he gets up early and before I'm even out of bed, here he comes, a whoopin' an' a hollerin', with Mr. Bear hot on his heels. Both come a-chargin' into the cabin, and as Jimbo scrambles out the back window, he yells: 'Skin that critter out, ol' buddy, while I go round up another'n.'"

The audience howled. Howard grinned, and promising the Bow Scouts he'd "not miss more'n a few hundred times," he warmed up by shooting a dozen arrows into the center of the on-stage target almost quicker than the eye could follow. He then popped a few balloons, knocked three ping-pong balls off their toothpick perches and pinned, with one arrow, a golf ball on a string that was swinging back and forth like a pendulum. After the applause died down, Howard took a break from shooting and described his tackle. He used Port Orford cedar arrows— although he quickly admitted that aluminum were better— because wood had more "romance" to it, and fletched each shaft with three, six-inch-long white feathers. His semi-long bow was made of split bamboo from Japan, laminated with fiberglass, and weighed sixty-five pounds at his 28 inch draw. He wore a cordovan leather shooting glove and a back quiver made of heavy, pliable latigo leather that conformed to the shape of his back, thereby cutting down the rattle of his arrows— "real necessary, brother, when you're out in the field an' don't want ol' Papa Bear to know you're tracking him."

His shooting style was fluid and easy to watch. In his now-familiar stance, he held the bow canted to his right, his body leaned slightly forward, left shoulder hunched over a little and the bow arm slighty bent, drawing the arrow back and anchoring for a split second alongside his cheek, with his release-hand middle finger touching a hole where an eyetooth used to be, and releasing so fast it seemed as if he didn't come to a complete stop.

When he was through describing his tackle and shooting technique, Howard turned to Steve and said, "All right, brother, start a-tossin' them coins."

It was Steve's job tonight to toss up coins so Howard could shoot them out of the air. It wasn't Steve's first time at this, and the young blond-haired man in his late twenties had learned to toss the coins so they didn't spin too much and gave Howard a chance to hit the flat side.

Six quarters, six hits.

Three dimes, three hits. Heck, it was almost monotonous. Finally, a missed dime (probably deliberate, Steve thought; done just to show everyone that what Howard was doing wasn't a cinch), then three more hits and Howard was satisfied that he hadn't lost his fine edge.

Then Howard paused, cut off the applause with a wave of his hand, and gave a little history on himself. "I was born on this big ol' cotton plantation in Shelby, Alabama...one of five young'ns—

Howard performed the feats in "Robin Hood."

all boys, I might add—started shootin' a bow at the ripe old age of four, killed my first rabbit at five, and knew somehow, even then, that archery would always be my first love. 'Course, I have to tell you. . .baseball ran it a close second on more'n one occasion, but somehow archery always won out and eventually became my ticket to a fair amount of success. . ."

Everyone listened, enthralled, as Howard continued with some of his hunting exploits, most of which were filmed and enjoyed by audiences the world over. American buffalo, grizzly, moose, deer, antelope, the big cats, rhino, even the mighty elephant—all have fallen victim to Howard's bow and arrow. There was the incredible story of a duck shot at 160 yards; an elk killed at 185 yards; and a bird shoot that took place at the pheasant club in Lone Pine in which Howard, using regular hunting arrows, not flu-flus (birds arrows with special wire attachments to insure easier hits), downed five birds with seven arrows. And all these stories told in such a wryly humorous, self-effacing manner that it was obvious Howard wasn't bragging. . .or trying to make himself seem larger than life; on the contrary, if one didn't listen carefully, and realized just how difficult and dangerous many of his shots were, one would come away feeling that Howard, far from being the greatest bowhunter who ever lived, had gained most of his reputation on pure luck—a "good ol' boy" archer who just happened to be in the right place at the right time.

And, of course, nothing could be further from the truth.

Now, with the evening wearing down, it was question and answer time, with many of the older members of the audience wanting to hear how Howard performed the feats in the Errol Flynn movie "The Adventures of Robin Hood."

Howard reflected a moment, thinking back on his early movie days, then launched into a wonderful anecdote about how worried at first the extras were at the idea of "some clown who thinks he's William Tell" shooting at them with "real" arrows!

"They weren't none to happy about it, let me tell you," Howard said, chuckling. "In fact, right off the bat most of 'em just disappeared real fast whenever I showed up. But after a spell, when they'd watched me do a few trick shots—you know, like splittin' an arrow, cuttin' the rope that Robin Hood was gonna be hung by, or shootin' this fella from horseback who was ridin' full-tilt after me in Sherwood Forest—and nobody got hurt, well, they began to relax an' finally, as the picture went on an' I never missed, most of the extras were always comin' up to me an' askin' when it was their turn to be shot!"

And so it goes...

Finally, after two hours, with Howard shooting or talking almost nonstop, it was time to end the demonstration. It was getting late and some of the parents were signaling that their youngsters had to be in bed.

Regrettably, the evening ended—all too soon for most of the audience. Autographed copies of Howard's two books, "Hunting the Hard Way" and "Wild Adventure" were eagerly purchased by the guests, and as they filed out of the auditorium, every awed youngster shook the hand that drew the string that shot the arrow that killed the...well, you know the feeling.

Afterward, in the now-empty auditorium with Howard talking to his long-time friend, Doug Easton, Steve gathered up Howard's portable target, bow, arrows and other archery tackle and carried everything out to his vehicle.

Outside, as Steve was packing everything away, the street light illuminated the nickname written under the fiberglass of Howard's bow. Knowing that Howard had a pet name for every bow he ever made, Steve wondered what the story behind this one was.

"How come you named this bow 'Little Sister'," he asked Howard when he joined Steve at the rear of the vehicle.

"Well, partner," he replied, "as you know, I don't have any children, an' I only got a mess of brothers...so when I made this cute little rascal—well, she felt so good in my hand, an' shoots so straight for me, I just naturally figured she was the kind of sister I'd always wanted. No," he added as Steve started to carefully put the bow into the back of his wagon. "You keep it, partner."

"But it's one of your favorite bows," Steve said, stunned.

"That's why I want you to have it," Howard said, gently. "That's what friendship's about—giving the folks you like things that mean a lot to you." And giving Steve a warm, thunderous pat on the back, he climbed into his vehicle and drove away.

It was a moment that Steve never forgot.

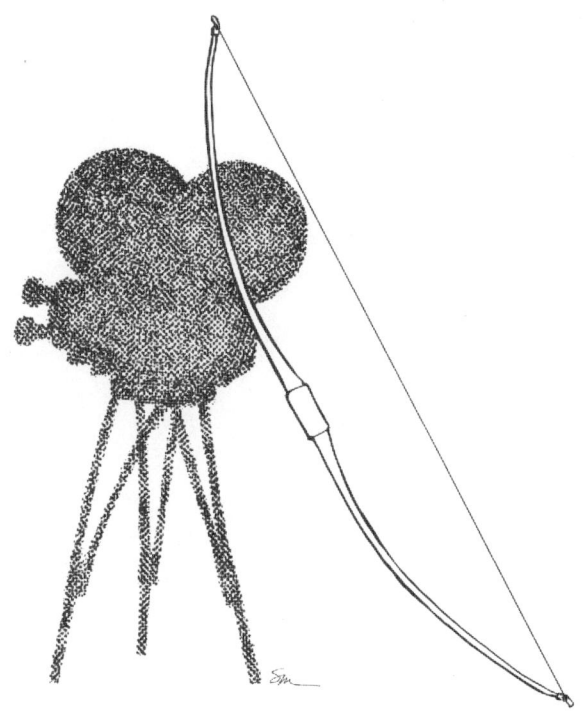

The Bushmen who live and hunt in the Kalahari Desert today lead a harsh, primitive life that is almost unchanged from that of their ancient ancestors. This may sound surprising, even dismaying to those of us who inhabit the rest of the supposedly civilized world.

But the Bushmen, who at one time peopled much of Africa... and are the oldest race on earth...are truly in tune with nature and would have it no other way.

THE BUSHMEN

FOR THREE WEEKS the hunters had found no game. Now, on the morning of the twenty-second day, the half-starved men gathered outside the hut of the medicine man, Nsomi, to receive his spiritual guidance.

Nsomi was a tiny, terribly wrinkled old Bushman whose yellow-brown flesh hung in great sagging folds that resembled ancient parchment. His thinning white hair curled into tight peppercorns, and his sparse, white goatee was stained with tobacco juice. Like all Bushmen he had slanted eyes, high cheekbones and a broad, flat nose.

No one knows how these original inhabitants of Africa inherited their distinct Mongolian features; or where the race originated. Legends told of long treks across Africa from unknown origins, and cave and rock paintings throughout Northern Africa indicated that at one time in the distant past Bushmen lived there. But over the eons other, stronger tribes had driven the friendly, peaceful Bushmen farther and farther south until now the survivors were scattered about the scorched, arid wastelands of the Kalahari Desert. Here, they practiced their primitive methods of hunting and gathering, leading the same nomadic life they had always led since before the Stone Age.

Game in the Kalahari was usually available, if not plentiful. Even during the summer, when there was no rain and the great herds of gemsbok, wildebeest, eland and impala trekked north in search of water, there were generally porcupines, snakes, lizards and other small game available; also, the women could be counted on to dig up edible roots and to uncover grubs or ants' eggs or caterpillars that when roasted were savory morsels. But there had been little rain that winter, and now in the white heat of summer the parched, cracked, sunbaked earth seemed devoid of all life.

Nsomi, seeing how weak and depressed the hunters were, knew he would have to cast his stongest spell over them to revive their flagging spirits.

Opening his "magical" leather bag, he took out two fire sticks. Inserting one stick through a hole in the other, the ancient medicine man twirled them between his palms and soon had smoke curling up from a bed of dry grass. He then threw tufts of leopard fur, the legs of the deadly yellow spider and powdered rhinoceros horn into the fire. The smoke thickened and a few tiny flames flickered. Satisfied, Nsomi motioned to the four hunters and, as one, they held out their left hand to Nsomi. He took a sharp flint from his bag, made a small incision in the palm of each hunter and motioned for them to hold the cut hand over the smoke. As they obeyed, Nsomi prayed to the Great Spirit, Gaua, who created everything, imploring him to bless the hunters and make this upcoming hunt successful.

Meanwhile, the smoke, in which Gaua existed, entered the soul of each hunter through the cut in their hand and filled each man with great hope. Rising, they thanked Nsomi for his good medicine and went to their makeshift grass huts. There, they collected their bows and poisoned-tipped arrows and headed out into the searing hot desert.

No one knew how long it had been since they had killed any game, for Bushmen cannot count past three; they just knew from the dull ache in their empty, extended bellies that they and their families were on the verge of starving, and they could not let another day pass without killing some sort of animal.

Ahead, the flat sandy desert was sprinkled with sun-withered grassy bushes whose ash-brown color contrasted sharply with the cloudless, eye-achingly brilliant blue sky. Here and there a few bleached Marula trees poked up through the pinkish-yellow sand and dunes crested with tufts of grass made up the distant horizon.

Led by Karnu, the oldest and wisest hunter, the Bushmen moved slowly over the hot sand. They seldom spoke, or gestured, preferring to conserve their energy for the hunt. The youngest, Sagai, carried his bow and a quiver of arrows slung over one shoulder so that his hands were free to carry an ostrich egg filled with water.

After following a dry riverbed for several hours, they paused under a large acacia tree. Here, between the roots, they buried the egg in a shallow hole to make sure they would have water on their return.

Continuing on across a wide sandy plain, the hunters paused every so often to look for game tracks. And whenever they came to a tall tree one of them climbed it and, eyes shaded against the blazing sun, looked in all directions for signs of life. But luck was still against them and it was midday before they found the tracks of a gemsbok in narrow, sandy gully.

The tracks were a few hours' old and led across the gully—becoming more apparent wherever the sand deepened—up the other bank and out across the open desert toward a clump of bushes visible a half-mile away.

The hunters smiled and nodded at each other, as if reassuring themselves that they were indeed following a live trail. As they pressed onward, each man nocked a poisoned arrow on his bowstring. A sense of tension spread among them. The Great Spirit had provided them with game and now it was their responsibility to make sure they didn't let it escape.

Fanning out, the Bushmen moved silently toward the bushes. Here and there the gemsbok's tracks showed faintly in the sand; at other times a broken twig, or a bent blade of grass told the alert hunters that their prey was straight ahead. As they drew near the bushes, Karnu signaled to Gogei and Nyika to work their way around behind the dense thicket and to be ready to shoot the gemsbok if it made a run for it. The two hunters moved off, bows and arrows held ready as they fixedly watched the bushes for any sign of the gemsbok.

Karnu and Sagai waited until their companions had disappeared behind the bushes, then inched forward themselves. They had to be close to their prey before they could risk a shot, for their little bows were too weak to cast an arrow accurately more than twenty yards. For this reason, they relied heavily on the poison smeared on their arrow points. It was so deadly, even the slightest scratch on an animal would cause eventual death.

Once among the bushes, however, the hunters faced another problem: even the smallest twig could deflect their arrows and cause them to miss their target. So they had to make sure they had a clear shot before releasing an arrow.

The bushes covered about a half-acre in area. Dense around the perimeter, they thinned out near the middle and then clumped together in a dense little thicket in the very center. As Karnu and Sagai approached the outer fringe of the bushes, they removed their quivers so that the gemsbok wouldn't be alerted by rattling arrows. Then, bows and arrows held ready to shoot, the two small gaunt Bushmen quietly eased their way through the bushes. Broken twigs and an occasional tuft of pale brown hair told the hunters that the gemsbok had entered this way. They moved forward even more carefully, scanning the bushes all around them for a glimpse of the gemsbok.

But the elusive animal wasn't in the dense outer bush. It was just beyond, standing in a small clearing, head in the sunburned grass, grazing. It was a fully mature buck gemsbok, with a horizontal black stripe separating the white belly from the brown upper body, and a black patch at the base of its long flowing tail. It had not heard the hunters approaching, but after a moment it lifted its head out of the grass and looked warily around, testing the hot, windless air for the scent of any foes. When it smelled no danger, it flicked its mulelike ears forward and listened. The sun glinted on its two upright, four-foot-long horns that swept slightly backward over its neck. In the white and black-marked face, the gentle brown eyes stared in the direction of the two motionless hunters. Then, not seeing them against the background of tangled bushes, the gemsbok lowered its head again and went on grazing.

Karnu and Sagai quickly drew their arrows back, aimed and shot at the gemsbok. The dull twang of both bowstrings alarmed the big buck. It jerked up its head, stiffening for an instant as the two arrows flew toward it. Then it leaped forward, out of the path of Sagai's poorly aimed arrow. But Karnu's shaft, aimed at the front of the belly, buried into the gemsbok's flank and the terrified animal carried it away as it crashed through the bushes ahead of the hunters.

Karnu and Sagai made no attempt to follow the gemsbok, but instead dropped their bows onto the grass and sat comfortably on their haunches. They knew that to chase the injured animal right away would only make it run farther; whereas if left alone, with no pursuit, the gemsbok would find the nearest available shade and lie down to die. So the two experienced hunters sat there, resting and smiling, knowing that the buck was as good as in their empty, aching stomachs.

Shortly, they were joined by Gogei and Nyika, who wanted to know what had happened. Karnu and Sagai explained briefly, gesturing and grunting, clicking their tongues and smacking their lips in the only language the primitive Bushmen knew—a language that cannot be written and is almost impossible for an outsider to duplicate or understand.

Gogei and Nyika were delighted by the news of the kill. Nyika removed the short wooden spear that he carried among the arrows in his quiver, and made several stabbing motions, as if killing the dying gemsbok. The others grinned and nodded their heads, pleased by Nyika's actions. Then all four hunters lay under a bush and took a short nap.

When they awoke some thirty minutes later, they moved out of the bushes and Karnu and Sagai gathered up their dropped quivers. Then, the four hunters fanned out and searched for the trail of the wounded gemsbok.

Shortly, they found a tiny splotch of blood on the burnt grass;

then another, and another. Excitedly, they followed the trail across the open desert for twenty minutes. Then Karnu stopped and pointed ahead at a half-grown Marula tree: under it, in what little shade existed in the blazing sun, lay the gemsbok. Its flight through the bushes had dislodged the Bushman's arrow, but blood seeped from the wound, staining the pale brown flank.

Although it was dying, and frothed at the mouth, the animal gamely staggered to its feet as it sighted the hunters and tried to run away. But its legs gave out and the big buck fell, legs splayed, on its face. Desperate, it struggled to its feet again, but didn't have the strength to move. Blood and froth spurted from its open mouth each time the animal breathed, and it quivered all over. But it gamely lowered its head, horns extended toward the hunters, and waited for death to strike.

The hunters closed in, still wary of the gemsbok's long sharp horns, and while Karnu, Sagai and Gogei kept the animal's frontal attention, Nyika moved in from the rear and stabbed his spear into the buck's heart. The gemsbok collapsed without a sound, made one final convulsive shudder on the ground...and died.

Quickly, the excited hunters cut up the dead buck with their flint skinning knives. They carefully cut away the flesh from around where Karnu's poisoned arrow struck, and threw the pieces aside. Already, vultures were circling high overhead and before long several of the big ugly birds had landed and were perched, hunched-over, bald heads thrust forward, eyes unwinkingly fixed on the kill, along the branches of a nearby dead tree.

The hunters ignored them. They had almost finished cutting up the gemsbok when a deep-chested, snarling roar made the Bushmen whirl around. There, crouched facing them some forty yards away, was a large, gaunt, black-maned lion.

Even as the hunters watched, motionless, the big cat inched forward, ears flattened, belly low to the ground, favoring its left front leg, which the hunters could see had been broken and hadn't healed properly so that below the first joint the paw stuck out at an unnatural angle.

After a few feet the lion stopped, only its long, black-tufted tail moving now, flicking sideways in the dirt, and gave a low, guttural snarl. Then it gathered its rear feet under its belly, hindquarters bunching, muscles rippling in the sunlight, and prepared to charge. Before it did it roared again, twisting its huge head from side-to-side in that jerky, half-sideways motion peculiar to all lions. Then it sprang, landing clumsily and off-balance without its front left paw to take the weight of its body but still moving fast, terrifyingly fast, coming in a half-limping, half-lumbering, heavy-bodied run that covered the forty odd yards separating him from the hunters almost faster than the eye could follow...or the mind could believe.

The hunters, motionless until now, suddenly scattered. They ran without looking back, in different directions, only stopping when each man knew the lion wasn't chasing him.

Some forty yards away, the hunters pulled up, chests heaving, and looked back at the lion and saw it had lost interest in them and was now lying with its head half-buried in the gemsbok carcass, devouring the flesh in great tearing gulps.

Karnu motioned for the others to join him behind a thornbush. Watchful of the lion's every movement, Sagai, Gogei and Nyika obeyed. Karnu indicated the lion, then with several tongue clicks and lip-smacking grunts, explained that they couldn't let the lion drive them away from their kill. Their families would die if the hunters returned without meat, and Karnu was not about to let that happen—even if it meant sacrificing his own life to accomplish his goal. The others agreed with him. They knew their weak bows couldn't bury their arrows deep enough to kill the lion instantly, or even swiftly enough for them to escape the big cat if it chose to charge them. But hunting and feeding their families was their role in life, and with game so scarce not one of them dared suggest that they move on and look for another kill.

Spreading out, the four hunters quietly closed in on the lion. The big cat paid no attention to them. Due to its crippled front paw, it too was on the verge of starvation and presently food was uppermost on its mind. It tore ravenously at the gemsbok carcass. Nearby, some of the braver vultures had left the branches of the dead tree and were now gathered in a semi-circle a few feet in back of the lion.

The hunters stopped when they were within twenty yards of the lion and motioned to each other that they were ready to shoot. Karnu gave the signal to fire. Each man took careful aim and shot a poisoned arrow at the lion. One shaft missed, the rest sank into the exposed rump of the lion. It sprang to its feet, roaring in rage and pain, pawed at the arrows sticking in its rump, then charged the hunters. They fled in different directions, hoping to confuse the lion long enough for them to reach the safety of some distant trees.

It might have worked, too, for the lion was too crippled to run far. But after only a short distance, Karnu stumbled and went sprawling. The breath was knocked out of him and before he could scramble to his feet, the lion was on him. It crushed his skull with one swipe of its paw, killing him instantly, then chewed and mauled the old Bushman beyond recognition. The other hunters continued running without realizing Karnu had fallen. Only when they had reached their chosen trees, climbed into the lower branches and "counted heads," did they see Karnu wasn't with them. They quickly looked back at the lion and saw it chewing on Karnu's mangled remains. Appalled, they shouted curses at the lion and begged the Great Spirit, Gaua, to receive Karnu's soul with honor and to treat their brave friend with much kindness and dignity. Then they got comfortable on the branches of their separate trees and waited, knowing that shortly the lion would die and they would be able to return to their families with enough meat to last them for many weeks.

The black-maned lion, meanwhile, dragged Karnu's mangled remains back beside the gemsbok carcass that was now smothered in hungry, squabbling vultures.

Enraged, the lion charged the feathered carrion-eaters, scattering them, chasing them away with loud, deep-chested roars. Then, wearied by the exertion, the big tawny cat stood there a moment, panting in the hot sun, tail switching, confused by the strange, numbing sensation that had already settled into its hindquarters.

Attracted by the lion's roaring, a lone jackal now trotted up and joined the circle of vultures sitting waiting for the lion to leave its kill.

And presently, as the lion grew weaker and slowly sank onto its trembling hindquarters, up loped a hyena, strings of drool dangling from its enormously powerful jaws.

Now all the characters in this wilderness play were present. And Nature, as it had since time immemorial, began taking its course...

While high, high overhead in the nude blue African sky, a commercial jetliner roared on its way south to Cape Town...its passengers drowsily unaware of the primitive savagery that was taking place far, far below them on the sands of the Kalahari Desert.

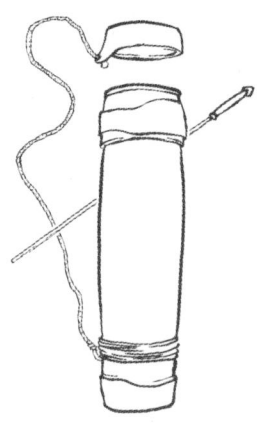

> "The most important thing in the Olympic Games is not to win but to take part, just as the most important thing in life is not the triumph but the struggle. The essential thing is not to have conquered but to have fought well."
> —Baron Pierre de Coubertin,
> Founder of the International Olympic Committee and re-establishment of the modern Olympic Games

THE OLYMPIANS

IN 1920, DUE TO lack of interest among participating nations, the Olympic committee decided to drop archery from the Olympic Games. All attempts to get the sport reinstated in the next two Olympic Games failed, so in 1931 archery enthusiasts in Belgium, France and Poland formed the Federation Internationale de Tir a l'Arc (F.I.T.A.). They were greatly concerned that archery was not an Olympic sport, and the primary goals of F.I.T.A. were to carry out the ideals of the Olympic image. But, despite F.I.T.A.'s efforts, archery in the 30's and 40's was still not popular with the general public, who, worldwide, preferred such sports as baseball, football, boxing, cricket and soccer. Only a small select group, comprised mainly of professional men who had more time for leisure as well as the money to afford expensive, hard-to-get equipment, kept the sport of archery alive.

After World War 11, thanks to Howard Hill's exciting skills in popular movie shorts and public demonstrations, archery slowly began to catch on with the masses. Also, due to manufacturers

Munich was soon pulsating with Olympic fever.

like Fred Bear, Ben Pearson, Earl Hoyt and the Wilson brothers, whose bows were technically advanced, and James "Doug" Easton, the "father" of the aluminum arrow, archery scores climbed and with them so did the interest of the general public.

It took a decade for archery to really grow popular. But by the late 50's, archery was considered to be the world's fastest growing sport; and in 1961, the thirty-five member nations of F.I.T.A. elected an indomitable English spirit named Mrs. Inger Frith to be their president.

Mrs. Frith and her staff worked tirelessly over the ensuing years to get archery re-established in the Olympics. It was a difficult task, for although archery was popular it was still overshadowed by many other sports that were vastly more exciting to watch. Finally, however, F.I.T.A. persuaded the Olympic Committee to include archery in the 1972 Games to be held in Munich, Germany.

Munich, an 800 year old city rebuilt from the rubble of the Blitz of World War 11, was soon pulsating with Olympic fever, and its citizens warmly welcomed all the visiting athletes.

The archery tournament was held in the beautiful English Gardens, a short distance from the Olympic track and field stadium. The four-day event was for men and women, and ninety-six archers from twenty-seven nations competed. Archers were housed with the other athletes in the Olympic Village, and bused daily to the tournament site.

For the first few days of the Games, archers spent their time on the practice field or in town sight-seeing. But then the morning they had all been waiting for arrived, and the archers entered the English Gardens for the first day of competition.

The tournament field was in immaculate condition, while in the background the decorative flags of the various competing nations fluttered proudly in the warm breeze.

A German band, resplendent in their gray and gold-trimmed uniforms, played a repertoire of festive music, welcoming everyone to the opening ceremonies.

Mrs. Frith and other F.I.T.A. officials sat watching the competition from under a big orange awning erected over a raised platform facing the field. During the tournament they were joined by many visiting dignitaries, such as Prince Carlos of Spain, Willie Dorm, president of the organizing committee for the Olympic Games, and Olympic president, Avery Brundage.

Because the archers shot in the morning and the afternoon for four consecutive days, umbrellas were set up along the shooting line to shade the competitors from the sun. Men and women wore their customary white attire, which also helped keep them cool in the mid-afternoon heat.

On the field, the official score-keepers relayed by portable telephone the individual scores of each archer to the scoreboard crew, who posted the scores of the top ten men and women archers on a huge board following each end.

The competition between the archers of different nations was tense and exciting, and drew huge galleries every day. John Williams of the United States gradually pulled away and won the gold medal, with Gunnar Jervill of Sweden, and Kyosti Laasonen of Finland taking the silver and bronze medals, respectively. In the women's competition, American Doreen Wilbur finally beat out Irena Szydlowska of Poland for the gold medal, while Emma Gaptchenko of the Soviet Union hung on to get the bronze.

But more important than the competition, the world record scores, or even the winning of medals, was the camaraderie among the archers.

For after thousands of years of war, bows and arrows were at long last not being used by human beings to kill each other, but in the spirit of competition—men and women from all parts of the world contesting for peaceful goals, as friendly rivals rather than bitter enemies.

The bow and the arrow are part of mankind's ancestry, a legacy from prehistoric times that will always be around. Let us hope we can say the same for mankind, itself.

STEVE HAYES was born in London, England. In 1950 he moved to Los Angeles and began an acting career in movies, television and on the stage. In 1958 he fought in the Cuban revolution and in 1961 in the Belgian Congo uprising. A world traveler, he has explored the Amazon by boat, dug for gold in Alaska, and trekked in the Himalayas. He has been deeply involved in archery for thirty years, participating in National/International tournaments, teaching the US Special Forces and coaching archers who went on to compete in the Olympics. A writer since 1957, he is the author of THE OSPREY DILEMMA and has written numerous feature films (including *Time After Time* with Karl Alexander), television movies (*The Long White Summer, Young Buffalo Bill*) and mini-series (*The Seekers, Condominium*). Steve Hayes spent two years of painstaking research in preparing to write THE THIRD INVENTION, to make every incident as close to historical truth as possible. This research uncovered many little known facts, from the exact origin of ancient Chinese thumb rings and use of Turkish bows to the role Alexander the Great played in introducing archery to India. Steve also worked closely with the artist during illustration, to insure that every drawing in this book is historically and factually accurate.

NED DAMERON is an artist who is equally at home drawing and sculpting. His commercial work is primarily in book illustration. His book covers have appeared from Doubleday, Arbor House, Tor, Underwood-Miller and Donald M. Grant. He has storyboarded feature films and painted posters for the New Orleans Opera. Ned's work has been exhibited in galleries in New Orleans, Chicago, New Britain and San Francisco. He lives in Silver Spring, Maryland. Tailpiece art is by Sherrell Medberry.

Text was set in 11 point Baskerville, from Bitstream, Inc., Cambridge, Massachusetts. Benguiat titles were originated through Gem Artline, from Digital Research, Monterey, California. Type was set with Xerox Ventura Publisher and Professional Extension, from Xerox Corporation, Dallas, Texas, using an LX6 Professional Controller, from LaserMaster Corporation, Eden Prairie, Minnesota. Books were printed and bound by The Lakeside Press, R.R.Donnelley & Sons Company, Harrisonburg, Virginia.